THE LEARNING CIRCLE

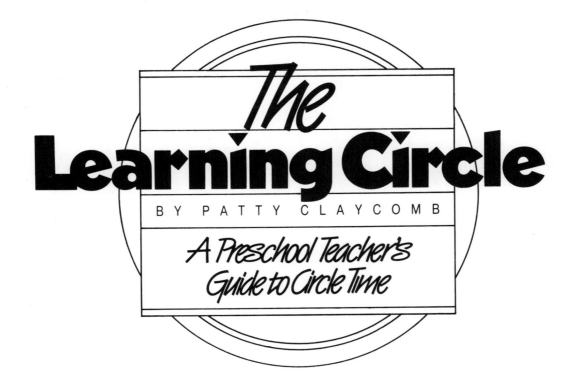

The Learning Circle

BY PATTY CLAYCOMB

A Preschool Teacher's Guide to Circle Time

GRYPHON HOUSE, INC.

MT. RAINIER, MARYLAND

© 1988 by Patty Claycomb
ISBN 0-87659-115-2
Library of Congress Card Catalog Number: 88-80523

Published by Gryphon House, Inc., 3706 Otis Street,
Mt. Rainier, Maryland 20712.

Cover illustration: Annie Lunsford
Design: Graves, Fowler & Associates
Typesetting: Lithocomp

Dedicated to my parents, Dr. Charles and Ruth Jones, who taught me to weave the magic of childhood into my life and to my husband Robert and my daughters Rachael and Wendy who bring me constant joy.

TABLE OF CONTENTS

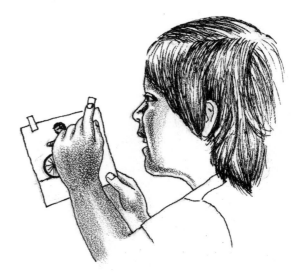

THE LEARNING CIRCLE

TABLE OF CONTENTS

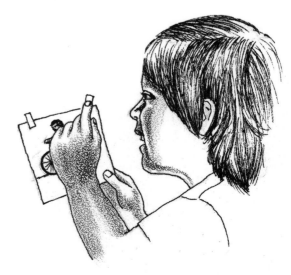

CHAPTER FOUR
BRAINSTORMS

INTRODUCTION

Welcome to a Learning Circle. It is a circle of children. Within this circle many exciting things will happen. Learning to think will ignite an air of wonder. Minds will sparkle and stretch! New worlds of discovery will open up. The doorway to these new worlds is a fun and exciting Learning Circle.

To present material to a circle of children is an easy task. To present material so that it is captivating and the magic of learning is alive is a more difficult task. To do this, the material and presentation should focus on how children think, feel, and react to their surroundings. Consider the following questions. Will this experience provide a child with information to think and wonder about? Is it fun? Learning and having fun is the magic of a Learning Circle. Does the experience inspire imagination? Will this encourage the child to learn more? Is curiosity encouraged? Can questions be asked? Are there discoveries? Are the children full of wonder and amazement?

The materials for the activities in this book are simple and easily obtained. This makes them easy for teachers and for parents to do at home. Many activities use felt pens. They add bright visual stimulation. With just a few other simple materials like posterboard, scissors, tape, and crayons, many exciting times are waiting for the children at the Learning Circle.

The Learning Circle activities are grouped into the following categories: The Seasons, Music and Movement, Learning Circle Games, The Senses, Communication, and Crafts. Activities for the older preschool child are presented in The Human Body, Nutrition, The Ocean, Land Forms, Plants, Space, The Planets, Prehistoric Life, and Inventions. The activities will challenge a child to think and imagine! Children thrive on mental stimulation, especially if it is fun. Children learn through active involvement. Watch their minds grow, their vision sharpen. Watch them make exciting discoveries with the entire class participating! Interest remains high and minds stay focused on the experience.

Call a Learning Circle! The children are waiting.

TEACHING TECHNIQUES

TEACHING TECHNIQUES

The teacher is the heart of the classroom. Working with the curriculum in a creative setting, the teacher makes the program successful. Discovering what makes each child so different and helping each child develop to his or her potential are two of the many challenges and responsibilities of the teacher. Others include: to understand and meet the needs of each child; to provide an atmosphere that is safe and trusting; and to develop a method of teaching within the Learning Circle that is conducive to learning.

UNDERSTANDING EACH CHILD

Each child has different needs and characteristics. A number of teaching techniques can help the teacher discover the individual characteristics of each child. The following techniques can be modified as needed.

Bear Hugs. A Bear Hug is a good activity to learn about the children and to help them learn about each other. Prepare a box with a selection of questions inside. Call the children to a Learning Circle. The teacher selects a child to answer a question. This child chooses a question from the box. If this is a start of the year Bear Hug, the questions might read:
- What is your favorite color?
- What do you like to eat?
- What is your favorite thing to do?
- What makes you happy?
- Who is in your family?
- Do you have any pets?
- What do you want to be when you grow up?

Since children are eager to talk about themselves, begin this activity with two or three children. More children and questions can be added in subsequent Bear Hugs.

Bear Hugs can follow a special holiday or event. Vacation Bear Hugs are very popular! Suggested questions are:
- What did you do on your vacation?
- Did you travel someplace else?
- How did you get there?
- Did someone visit you?
- What did you do that was fun?

Bear Hugs are helpful in many ways. They provide a surprising amount of information about each child throughout the year. They satisfy a basic need to be heard and teach the children how to wait and listen. They help to develop the ability to express oneself.

Special Time Activities are geared towards making a child feel special. An example is *The New Shoe Song*. The child with new shoes walks around the Learning Circle while everyone sings The New Shoe Song to the tune of "Mary Had A Little Lamb."

Someone here has new shoes on,
New shoes on, new shoes on.
Someone here has new shoes on
And that someone is you!

Clean and bright and looking good,
Looking good, looking good.
Clean and bright and looking good,
The way that new shoes should.

Spotlight Time. The parents of a specific child are asked for a brief description of their child's favorite food, toy, television show, and even a humorous event. At the Learning Circle the teacher describes this child and the children guess who the mystery person is. Each child has a turn during the year. This technique allows a teacher to give a child an extra dose of recognition.

Personal Bear Hugs. The children can ask to have a Personal Bear Hug when they have something special to tell or when there is something they would like to express to the whole class. It might be about a recent vacation, the birth of a new family member, or a newly acquired pet. A Personal Bear Hug makes a child feel special and develops communication within the classroom.

Observation. By watching the children and seeing their behavior and play, the teacher gains invaluable information. Perhaps there is a child who becomes frustrated when trying to talk to the teacher or a child who pulls away from the teacher when the teacher touches him or her. The children's behavior will provide the teacher with clues concerning their individual needs. Maybe one child needs more confidence and a better self-image. If a child is not comfortable with physical contact, develop a relationship that is suitable for this child. A child's inability to express himself or herself can stem from many sources. Discover the source of the trouble.

Group needs will also surface through observation. For example, a group of children on a daily basis played with a set of small toys. They would crawl under a table or squeeze behind any large structure they could find. It became obvious that they wanted an area separate from the rest of the classroom. After making a space for them to play, they never moved and they no longer left toys behind the bookcase or hiding in cubbies!

Listening. The children will tell the teacher many of their own needs. If a child is telling a story, listen closely! Perhaps this child needs the teacher's undivided attention. Another child may be telling the teacher that no one is friendly. And yet another is asking for a third hug at nap time because he or she needs extra reassurance. The children's questions and demands provide the teacher with invaluable information. Sometimes the need is simple. At other times the teacher must look below the surface to find the real need.

Individual Time. When a child asks the teacher to play a card game, take advantage of this request. When another child clings to the teacher's side, this is an opportunity to learn more about this child. The teacher can ask a child who has difficulty counting to play a special board game. Part of teaching is getting to know the children and tending to their needs.

A SAFE AND TRUSTING ATMOSPHERE

Providing an atmosphere where a child feels safe and secure is a primary need. The classroom is like a home. There is an authority figure, a set of rules, certain rituals that are observed, and a group of people who socialize and communicate. Rituals and routines help to create a safe and secure feeling. When they are performed on a daily basis or often enough so that the children know what to expect, they are a source of comfort. Below are some activities to encourage a safe and friendly feeling in the classroom.

A Getting To Know You Song. When the children learn about their surroundings, they will begin to feel more secure. Singing *A Getting To Know You Song* in the Learning Circle will encourage this feeling. This song can be used throughout the year, but especially when a new child enters the class. The tune is "The Itsy Bitsy Spider."

Here we are together, together, together,
Here we are together in our nursery class.
There's _____, and _____, and _____, and _____,
and _____, and _____, and _____, and _____.

Insert a child's name in each blank. When the children become familiar with this song, point to each child as their name is sung. This technique will help the children learn each other's names.

Body Tracing. Large pieces of butcher paper and a group of children are all that is needed. The children lie down on the paper and their bodies are traced and cut out. The children color their outline, adding their own face, hair, and clothing. Then the outlines are displayed on the wall with hands joined. Their names are printed large and clear on each body. The children enjoy seeing each other on the wall and learn to recognize the names of all the children. The paper people encourage the first trickle of social interaction within a new classroom.

Roll Call Noises. This is a good ritual to begin the morning. It starts the day with a laugh and sets a nice friendly mood for the Learning Circle. When taking the roll tell the children that they can respond with a word or noise. Reinforce the idea that it should be a friendly word or noise, not a screaming one. The following conversation is an example of Roll Call Noises.

Teacher: Michael, are you here?
Child: Boo!
Teacher: We have a classroom ghost! I hope you are friendly. Thank you, Michael.

Teacher: Margo.
Child: Bunny.
Teacher: That is a nice word, Margo. You have a pink bunny on your T-shirt.

Teacher: Mary, are you with us today?
Child: California.
Teacher: Good word, Mary. We have been talking about that state in our Learning Circle.

Teacher:	Nicky.
Child:	Roooooooooar!
Teacher:	What a sound! That could be a lion or a hungry dinosaur.

Teacher:	Paula.
Child:	A scratching sound on the rug.
Teacher:	Good sound, Paula. That is the first scratching sound in our Learning Circle.

Teacher:	Sharon, good morning. Are you here today?
Child:	No answer.
Teacher:	I can see a smile. I am glad you are with us today.

Teacher:	Meg.
Child:	Here.
Teacher:	Thank you for your nice here, Meg. It is a quiet word that I like to hear.

Roll Call Noises serve a number of purposes: they are great tension breakers with a new class; they stimulate the imagination; they encourage a quiet child to make a noise in front of the class for the first time; they provide an opportunity to recognize and compliment each child; and they can constitute a quick memory game. Don't forget to mention this ritual to a substitute. This teacher may have never experienced Roll Call Noises and may question the sanity of the children!

Crazy Week. This is a one minute ritual that takes place at the Learning Circle each day for one week. Monday is Monster Monday. For one minute everyone can make silly monster faces at each other, including the teacher. Tuesday is Tickle Tuesday. The teacher will surprise everyone with a quick tickle during the Learning Circle, without advance notice. Wednesday is Wiggle Wednesday. For one minute, wiggle! A less wiggly Learning Circle should result. Thursday is Thinking Thursday. Have everyone close their eyes and think of an object that the teacher suggests. This object could be an animal, something to eat, an object from home, or even a color. Have everyone open their eyes and, in turn, tell what picture came into their minds. This game is not only fun, but it also asks the children to use their memory while developing their ability to form mental images. Fun Friday is a day long ritual. If a good effort is made to observe the everyday rules during the week, certain rules are ignored on Fun Friday. The following are some examples:

- You may lay down and listen instead of sitting up during the Learning Circle.
- You may take off your shoes during indoor play.
- You do not have to line up to leave or enter the building.
- It is joke day! Jokes are shared at the Learning Circle. Knock-Knock, Elephant, and Monster jokes are well-liked by the children. The ability to understand a joke shows higher reasoning skills.
- It is sticker day. The children choose from a selection of stickers. If Astronomy is the topic of learning use space stickers. The best nappers for the week are allowed to pick first.
- Surprises such as a new toy or brownies for snack are saved for Fun Friday.

Classroom Tree. This is a ritual that is observed at the start of each month. It helps to introduce each new month and adds a change of decor to the classroom. A classroom tree can be made from a tree drawn on a posterboard, a branch secured in a container, or even a small plastic Christmas tree.

The children decorate the tree using a different theme each month. For January, they can draw and cut out happy faces to greet the new year. For February, a heart tree or cherry tree would be fun! For March, decorate the tree with rainbows and pots filled with gold.

Share Decisions. Give the children a limited amount of control over the events of the day and it will increase their feelings of security. Ask their opinions! Take votes by raising hands. Share ideas with them for possible activities. Ask for their ideas. Let them know that how they feel makes a difference.

Consistency. The teacher is the main source of a safe and trusting feeling. In order to provide this feeling the teacher's behavior, mannerisms, and reactions should remain the same. Be the same teacher on Monday as on Friday. Let the children know what to expect.

FORMING AND MAINTAINING A LEARNING CIRCLE

Trying to get the attention of a large group of children is a teacher's daily challenge. By engaging them through the senses of sound and sight the teacher can capture the interest of the children. Then the teacher can proceed with the Learning Circle. The following are attention-grabbers that can be used as often as necessary!

Sing A Song. Once the children recognize the tune, they will join in. The words of the song can signal the beginning of the Learning Circle and the movements can be used to bring the children where they need to be in the classroom.

Who Can Do What I'm Doing? Shake your hands, flex your feet, or rub your head and stomach at the same time.

What's In My Pocket? After a minute of wild guessing, show the object. A suggestion is a small toy mouse. The quietest child in the Learning Circle can hold the mouse.

Create A Distraction! Shake a box of pennies or marbles or shake a bag full of tin cans or rocks. At the end of the Learning Circle the children can guess what is making the noise.

What Is This? Show an object briefly and then quickly hide the object behind your back. The teacher can ask a surprise question about the object.

Jump Up And Down! Do jumping jacks or clap hands. Pretend to pick up an invisible animal and stroke it.

Hold Up an eye-catching picture, an amusing poster, or a humorous greeting card. The teacher can talk about the picture. At the end of the Learning Circle ask who can recall the picture.

Keeping interest alive is the magic of a Learning Circle. This magic is in material taught and how it is presented. Both contribute to the ultimate success of a Learning Circle. The following are techniques to maintain interest in the Learning Circle.

Enthusiasm. The teacher's enthusiasm for the material will be evident. If the teacher is excited and interested, then the class will be and the children will gravitate towards the teacher and the material. Each child should feel that their presence is what brightens up the day.

Fun! When learning about the letter *S* act out different *S* words. Form a *S*illy Learning Circle and have everyone act *S*illy. Everyone *S*tomps their feet, *S*lurps down an imaginary bowl of *S*oup, *S*tands up and then *S*inks down to the floor, or moves in *S*low motion. Learning becomes fun!

Listening Games. The children listen for *S* words. When they hear an *S* word they clap their hands. If the subject is the ocean, ask them to slap their knees when they hear an ocean-related word. Interest and fun is a magic combination.

Sense Of Humor. Never presume that the day will go as planned!

Anticipation. Children love to know what is coming next. The promise of future fun and activities will spark an interest in the Learning Circle.

Motivation. Something extra for a finished project such as a penny, a sticker, or a balloon can provide the motivation that some children need.

Visual Aids. For example, when studying numbers hold up a colorful posterboard with many numbers printed on it. Each child can find the number that is being discussed and place a sticky star on it. If the subject is color, hold up an appealing picture with many different shades of color. The children, in turn, find the colors. Then take the picture away and ask who can remember one of the colors. If it is a review of the alphabet, display a large busy poster full of many different objects. Then the children can find an object that begins with the letter *B*, or *H*, or *W*, or someone can find an object that begins with the letter that comes first in their name.

THE PARTICIPANT-OBSERVER BALANCE

When does a teacher become involved and when does a teacher step back and become an observer? The answer lies in the specific needs of the children, the situation, and in developing a teacher-intuition, formed through experience in the classroom. The children themselves will often provide clues concerning the role of the teacher in the classroom.

When introducing a group activity at the Learning Circle, the teacher's guidance is necessary to keep the activity flowing smoothly and fairly. Once the rules are understood, step back and give the children as much control as they can handle successfully. Guidance will still be necessary, but offer as few suggestions as possible.

Join the children in their play when it seems appropriate. Children need time to socialize without the presence or influence of an adult. Be close by to answer questions, compliment a task, or help with a problem. Observing the children at play is a fascinating learning experience for the teacher!

An argument is starting between two children. Observe. See if they can solve the problem together. One is starting to scream. Intervene. Tell this child that when he or she feels that angry to ask a teacher for help.

Participate when one child asks to play a card game. Observe when the children are playing with each other. Participate when one child has no one to play with. Observe when another child is sitting quietly playing with the dinosaurs. Participate when one child is having trouble finding someone to turn the jump rope, but step back when another child volunteers, even though he or she is not a good turner. Participate when a child needs direction with a particular task, but observe when he or she tries to do it. Doing a task for a child is neither a help nor a learning experience.

TECHNIQUES FOR GENERAL CLASSROOM USE

Standing quietly in line seems to be an unnatural request. Try these suggestions. Soldiers! Upon hearing this word have the children stand straight, arms to their side and facing forward. Have them march out. Penguins! Have the children stand tall and waddle out. Caterpillar! Have the children stand still and then all take a step at the same time, using first the left foot and then the right foot. Standing in line can be fun!

Use this technique to discourage pushing in line. "If you push, you will cause a traffic accident! The person in front of you will hit the person in front of them. Then I will call a tow truck and move you to the end of the line."

Try this technique when a child is using a loud voice in the classroom. "That is an outside voice. Let's take the loud noise you are making, roll it up in a ball, and throw it out the window. Now it is waiting for you outside, and you can find it as soon as we go outside."

The following is a good response for a child who is running in the classroom. "You are on high speed when you are running! You need to be on low speed in the classroom. I will twist your earlobe once and you will be on low speed. When you are outside I will twist your earlobe twice and you will be on high speed. Then you can run all you want!"

THE CREATIVE SETTING

THE CREATIVE SETTING

The environment of the classroom can be a positive force in the development of the child. The setting should not only contribute to a pleasant atmosphere, but also encourage participation, positive social behavior, and creative thinking. Consider these questions when organizing a classroom.

Is the room clearly and distinctly organized?

Does the room have easy access to materials?

Will the space provide the experiences that the child needs?

Does the atmosphere of the classroom invite the child to explore?

Learning begins here with a well-planned setting, a natural stepping stone to creative thinking.

ROOM ARRANGEMENT

The classroom is a vehicle, a mode of transportation to exciting adventures. It should provide a place for children to play and learn creatively with enough space to comfortably develop social skills. The room itself will influence the options, but do not let physical limitations restrict creativity. Slide and push, rearrange and hang. Transform the classroom into an environment designed for children. Here are some possibilities.

Look For Well-Defined Areas Of Play: a quiet reading space, a science table to touch and observe, an art center, a kitchen area, a dress-up area, a space for building blocks, and tables designated for various games, puzzles, and small toys.

Arrange The Different Areas in the room so that a minimal amount of interference exists between each activity. A library needs a separate quiet space while a dress-up area can work well near the kitchen area since both are household related and tend to mesh together in play. The block area should be as separate as possible. A natural law of nature exists here—blocks that are built up eventually will fall down!

Use Different Colors to separate the room spaces. Bright yellow and orange can highlight a kitchen area. Colors that tend to calm behavior such as blues and greens can be used in a library. Color is a great mood creator. It also provides quick visual clues for movement within the classroom. Try hanging colorful signs above each area. A sign saying *Library* can hang over the book area. A picture of a favorite book or fairytale figure can provide an additional visual clue. *Home Sweet Home* can hang over the kitchen area. Hang *Imagination Station* over the art center or *Mother Nature's Corner* over the science table. Throw rugs in different colors or yarn taped to the floor can separate the play areas. Even if the room space is limited, imagination is not!

Create Play Areas that are unique. Drape a large sheet across two structures and secure tightly to form a Hide-a-Way space. Providing a place for privacy to look at a book or just to be alone can be a lifesaver to a child who feels a need to escape.

Create A Dressing Room for the dress-up area by draping a sheet from the ceiling. A full length mirror inside the sheet room adds to the fun. Watch classroom magic soar!

Is there plenty of elbow room? Many classrooms will have at least twenty-four elbows. If the room begins to feel crowded, move something out!

CLASSROOM DECOR

Decorations and designs can add a continuous spark of magic to the atmosphere in the classroom. Listed below are a variety of room designs to provide a wide range of learning experiences. Changing the room decor provides an opportunity to challenge minds and sharpen the senses.

Alphabet Letters on the wall can be used many times during the year, just add a little classroom magic to them. They can be made out of brightly colored posterboard and protected with contact paper. Hang them within reach and attach a small object to each letter. For example, on the letter *C*, the object can be a caterpillar made from colored pipe cleaners cut into two inch pieces. The children can trace the letters, become familiar with the shapes, and add imaginative play to the experience.

Fill a wall with matching pictures and words to create a *Word Wall*. Themes for a Word Wall can be animal pictures and names; community scenes and words such as walk, don't walk, stop, phone, danger, police, push, pull, and sale!; balloons and the matching color words; or print the names of the children on strips of colored posterboard. Self-portraits can be drawn next to their names. Periodic changes in the Word Wall will keep this space alive.

A Wallpaper Wall will challenge the interior decorators in the classroom. If it is Autumn, decorate a wall with colorful leaves taped to a posterboard. A variety of materials such as tin foil, cotton balls, macaroni, felt material, or jar lids can be used on this wall. Encourage the children to bring different materials from home.

A Birthday Wall will please everyone. Draw a large cake with many candles. Print the name of a child on every candle. When someone has a birthday give them a paper flame to place at the top of their candle. By the end of the year the cake will be lit! A variation is to use the middle of a flower and add petals each time a birthday is celebrated. Eventually, the flower will be completed. Each child can look forward to participating in the finished picture.

Hang a colorful sign which reads **Word For The Week.** This sign introduces new vocabulary words. Interesting words such as whale, shark, bat, star, or moon are exciting to learn about. If a letter is being highlighted, the word for the week can begin with that letter.

Postcards can make a colorful wall design, but it involves a certain amount of collecting! Enough cards to print names, shapes, or any other topic will be needed. Christmas and holiday cards, different colored envelopes, and colorful wrapping paper can also be used.

A helpful hint: Alphabet letters, signs, posters, cards, and many other materials can be preserved for use year after year with clear contact paper applied over the front and back.

MANIPULATIVE EXPERIENCE

The selection of toys and learning materials should spark young minds as much as any other part of the program. The materials offered should help to encourage creative play, develop fine motor skills, and focus on a variety of concepts such as classification, sorting, perceptual skills, and memory. There should be enough of each material to enable easy sharing. Good classroom organization is also important. Give the children specific instructions about where to play with the toys and material.

Continued interest in the classroom toys is an important element to consider. Begin each year with a good selection, but leave some of the material at home. Periodically introduce something new to keep the magic of discoveries alive. The following are possible play materials for use in the classroom. The materials are best kept in separate play boxes.

Basic Building Materials. This would include large wooden blocks, small square alphabet blocks, Legos, and bristle blocks. These are excellent building tools, not only for structures, but for imaginations as well.

Kitchen Materials. Offer a variety of kitchen materials for many choices of creative play. This can include a set of colorful dishes, cups and utensils, a set of pots and pans, plastic food items, a special box with cookie cutters and playdough for kitchen use only, a spatula, a hot pad, a cookie sheet, a three minute timer for baking, a small broom, an apron, and a feather duster.

Dress-Up Clothes. Offer a good selection to dress up the imagination! Skirts, long dresses, men's shirts, ties, hats, wigs, scarves, shawls, gloves, belts, shoes, and slippers are all-time favorites. Additional accessories can include necklaces, plastic hawaiian leis, head bands, and fans!

Books for the classroom library. Offer books that have large, colorful illustrations. They will draw the child into the book. The following are examples of books that are interesting and appealing to children.

The Wolf's Chicken Soup by Keiko Kasza.
Sunshine by Jan Ormerod.
Moonlight by Jan Ormerod.
Sleeping by Jan Ormerod.
I'm Going on a Dragon Hunt by Maurice Jones.
Humphrey's Bear by Jan Wahl.
The Teddy Bear's Picnic by Jimmy Kennedy.
Bird's New Shoes by Chris Riddell.
Hey, Al by Arthur Yorinks and Richard Egielski.
When the Sun Rose by Barbara Helen Berger.

Frosted Glass by Denys Cazet.
Little Rabbit's Loose Tooth by Lucy Bate.
Never Talk to Strangers by Irma Joyce.
The Very Hungry Caterpillar by Eric Carle.
Where the Wild Things Are by Maurice Sendak.
In the Night Kitchen by Maurice Sendak.
Rainbow Goblins by De Rico.
Animals Born Alive and Well by Ruth Heller.
Jog Frog Jog by Barbara Gregorich.
Elephant and Envelope by Barbara Gregorich.

A Dinosaur Box. This box contains a large assortment of colorful dinosaurs. Along with the dinosaurs, a large rubber bin partially filled with colored aquarium gravel can also be offered. In this bin the dinosaurs dig caves, attack, play, and bury themselves underground. The bin helps to keep them concentrated in one area instead of stomping around the room!

A Top Box. In this box is a selection of small tops and other toys that spin such as spools or wooden beads. These toys are great for developing fine muscle control. The box can also contain jacks, coins, jar lids, and small rubber balls for beginner spinners. These objects cause great excitement when they are spun for the first time. Even the twentieth spin provokes tremendous enthusiasm. Mastery of this skill is a real ego booster.

Kitten Counters. These can be purchased at most educational supply stores. There are one hundred colorful plastic kittens to a box. They can be used for imaginative play, sorting, and counting. They are extremely popular and often one hundred is not enough! Make the Kitten Counters a table toy or they will be found baking in the play oven or hiding in a dress-up shoe!

Magnets. These offer fascinating play for building magnetic structures and demonstrating the behavior of magnetized objects. As an option to purchasing a magnetic set, one horseshoe magnet and a box of paperclips attract as much attention.

Marbles. Marbles are full of magic! A large selection in different colors, patterns, and sizes are wonderful additions for play. Marbles are best offered under teacher supervision. They can be placed in a large bin for easy viewing or on the rug encircled by a piece of yarn. Sorting by color and size can be encouraged. Marbles are great for creative play, social interaction, and group discussions. The teacher can describe a particular marble and see who can find it. The children can increase their perceptual skills by describing marbles to each other.

A Penny Box. This box is filled with pennies and has a few nickels and dimes in it, too. The popularity of this box is challenged only by the marbles! The children can use the pennies to count, stack, and create various designs on a table. They also become familiar with the difference between a penny, a nickel, and a dime.

A Letter Box. This is a box that contains twenty-six objects each starting with a different letter of the alphabet. The objects are added one by one as each letter is discussed in class. The children can use the objects for creative play and, at the same time, are reminded of the letters that they have learned.

Classroom Creature. This is a box that contains a small stuffed animal. If the animal is a bear, the box will be labeled with the word *Bear*. Playing with and taking care of the Classroom Creature is an enjoyable responsibility. Once a month change the Classroom Creature and the label on the box. Anticipation and excitement over a new Classroom Creature stirs magic into the atmosphere of the classroom!

Dominoes and Puzzles. These provide opportunities for individual or group play. Giant floor puzzles create a giant amount of enthusiasm! Prepare storybook puzzles. Cut out the pages of a short, highly illustrated book, cover them with contact paper, and place them in a box. As the pages are placed in the right order, the story is retold, and sequencing skills are mastered.

Card Games. Card games are great learning tools! They encourage rule following and listening skills, sharpen memory, and develop good social skills. Every few months one or two new games can be introduced. Change keeps interest alive! The most popular games are *Go Fish, Old Maid, Concentration,* and *War*. These games are found at most toy stores. While they are a great source of enjoyment, they are also educational. Concentration teaches memory and recognition skills. War teaches the sequence of numbers, and higher and lower number concepts. Use contact paper to cover each playing card and these card games will survive the bites and bends of a school year.

Teacher-Directed Board Games. These board games offer great opportunities for teaching numerous concepts. They are best played on a one-to-one basis. Popular games are *The Original Memory Game, Potato Head Kids Game, Operation, Candyland,* and *Carebears Game*. These games can be found at most toy stores. Popular games that can be found at educational supply stores are *Dinosaur Lotto, Ocean Lotto, Jungle Lotto, Teddy Bear Bingo,* and games by Ravensburger such as *Off To The Tower, Fruit Basket, Make A Mouse,* and *Garden Surprise.*

An Art Table. This area can be used anytime during a free play period. A variety of art materials are placed within easy reach. The children can draw, color, or work with playdough. The art table is supervised during painting or gluing activities. Children can turn a drop of glue into a three inch blob in a matter of seconds!

Playdough. Large colorful mounds of playdough seem to be an absolute necessity in the classroom. A dough box filled with items such as plastic knives for cutting, small plastic animals, rolling pins, cake pans, cookie sheets, spatulas, popsicle sticks, plastic flowers, and an assortment of cookie cutters can only enhance the playdough experience. The following playdough recipe is always successful. When making mounds of playdough double the recipe!

Cooked Playdough: Mix all ingredients together and cook in a pan on top of the stove. Stir constantly. Cook until the dough pulls away from the sides of the pan.

1 cup flour
1/2 cup salt
2 TB cream of tartar
2 TB oil
1 cup water—with added food coloring.
Store the playdough in a covered container.

An effective arrangement of play materials is to label each shelf with a number and the play material with matching numbers. The children can check the number on their toy and place it back on the shelf with the matching number. This method helps to keep the shelves organized and the materials easy to locate. Number recognition is also encouraged. As an alternative label the shelves and toys with colors or shapes.

CLASSROOM JOBS

Classroom jobs are an important part of the pattern of the day. They are like friends with whom you feel safe and secure. They help to form a feeling of belonging and unity since they can involve the participation of the entire class. Classroom jobs can include line leader, teacher's helper, calendar marker, bell ringer for clean up, snack helpers, lunch helpers, and light monitor. While these are popular, classroom jobs can go far beyond line leader and teacher's helper. They can be creative learning adventures!

The **Classroom Calender** can be a creative experience. Cut out thirty-one circles from white construction paper. Number these circles on the bottom and place these circles on a sheet of paper. As the children mark each day have them draw a picture on each circle using a felt pen. A different concept can be used each month such as happy faces for September, hearts for February, ghosts for October, and suns for a summer month.

An enjoyable reading job can be **Animal Feeder.** Position a popsicle stick between the arms of a stuffed animal. Print a word on a strip of paper, punch two holes at the top of the paper, and with yarn tie the paper onto the stick. If the stuffed animal is a monkey, one child will be the Monkey Feeder for the day. After the child reads the word on the paper he or she can choose a dried banana chip from a box and place it in a bowl in front of the monkey. If the stuffed animal is a bird, feed it sunflower seeds! Change the animal and the word often for that element of surprise in the classroom.

Balloon Reader is sure to catch the attention of everyone. Blow up a balloon and print a word on it using a dark felt pen. Tape the balloon on a wall. Tie a string of yarn on the bottom of the balloon and let it dangle. Help the Balloon Reader sound out the word on the balloon. Then print the name of the Balloon Reader on an uninflated balloon. Have the child tape the balloon on the wall near the one that is blown up. When everyone has a balloon on the wall and has read the word, send their balloons home! As an option, display a helium balloon that has a word printed on it. Read the word often. The helium balloon will last a month. Its presence will spark instant magic in the classroom!

Moon Checker will encourage the recognition of many shapes. Draw a simple landscape of ground and trees on a sheet of white construction paper. Draw a shape in the sky and cover it with a small piece of paper. The child who is the Moon Checker will lift up the paper and identify the shape. This is the moon! If the shape is not a circle or a half moon then it is a moon shining over another planet. Ask the Moon Checker to think of a name for the strange planet. Choose a different Moon Checker each day.

Egg Counter will bring a touch of farming to the classroom. Place a stuffed chicken or a chicken cut from posterboard in a basket. Place a number of small styrofoam balls under the chicken. The child who is the Egg Counter that day will remove the chicken from her nest and count the number of eggs she has laid. After the eggs have been counted have everyone sound like a very proud chicken that has laid her eggs!

Some of the activities in Chapter Three can be introduced as daily classroom jobs. These activities are Sticker Person, Robot Reader, Bumper Sticker, and Wish Person. Offer a variety of classroom jobs throughout the year. Find the jobs that the class enjoys and offer them often.

RULES

A set of clearly defined classroom rules must be provided. Rules are the backbone of any successful program. They teach positive social behavior, discipline, and control. They provide guidelines for how one should act and react, and what kind of behavior is expected.

At the start of each year explain and discuss the rules of the classroom. The teacher can continue to remind the children during the first two weeks. After this time, there are no more warnings! Consistency and firmness bring out the very best behavior from the children.

EXAMPLES OF RULES:

- Sitting is best for listening at the Learning Circle.
- One person speaks at a time. When the teacher is talking, raise your hand if you have something to say.
- In the classroom only walking is allowed. Outside you may run all you want.
- Please keep everything in its own space. The room will stay neat and orderly and everyone will know where everything is!
- Inside the classroom please use an inside voice.
- Hurting someone is not allowed in the classroom.
- While you are standing in line please wait without pushing.
- At naptime the toy or animal from home may nap with you.

DAILY SCHEDULES

There are many possible schedules that can work successfully for nursery school and day care programs. The schedule will be influenced by the number of children participating, the temperament of the children, and the climate. The schedule should move from one activity to another without tiring the children physically or mentally. In the following schedule the Learning Circle activities are offered twice and have an ample amount of time between them. There is a play period offered before each sitting activity. Language development can be a quiet discussion on a chosen topic as this can set a nice mood for the lunch table. If possible, outside play before nap helps even the most wriggly child to relax. Offering two play periods before the first Learning Circle will have the same effect.

Time	Activity	Time	Activity
8:00 – 9:00	Free Play	12:00 – 12:30	Lunch
9:00 – 9:15	Snack	12:30 – 1:00	Outside Play
9:15 – 9:30	Clean Up	1:00 – 2:30	Story, Nap
9:30 – 10:15	Outside Play	2:30 – 3:00	Snack, Clean Up
10:15 – 11:00	Learning Circle: This can include roll call, classroom jobs, Learning Circle activities, and sharing.	3:00 – 3:30	Outside Play
		3:30 – 4:00	Art Activity
		4:00 – 4:30	Free Play
		4:30 – 4:45	Learning Circle: Review the day's happenings.
11:00 – 11:30	Free Play		
11:30 – 11:40	Clean Up	4:45 – 5:00	Story
11:40 – 12:00	Language Development: Discussions on the topic of study, ending with music, songs, fingerplays, rhythm activities, or stories.	5:00 –	Free Play

When designing a schedule allow for a certain amount of overlap within each time frame. A schedule is a guideline to help cover the information, ideas, and needs of the children for that day. It is not a hard, fast rule. Experiment! Find out what works best.

LEARNING CIRCLE
ACTIVITIES

SCHOOL HOUSE

MATERIALS

White posterboard, felt pens.

PREPARATION

Draw a large school house on the posterboard.

LEARNING CIRCLE ACTIVITY

1. The children sit in the Learning Circle and look at the empty school house.
2. Explain that autumn brings the start of a new school year with the promise of learning about many new things.
3. Have the children express their ideas about what they would like to learn.
4. Each child chooses a felt pen and draws, in the school house, a picture of something they would like to learn about in school.
5. As the school house fills up with flowers, rainbows, rocketships, and dinosaurs, the children will see that many exciting experiences are in store for them.

EXPANDING KNOWLEDGE

Discuss the pictures that have been drawn and then turn the school house around. Se who can remember the pictures.

MATERIALS FOR TEACHING TIPS

Felt pens, pennies, tape.

TEACHING TIPS

Add a promise! Have the children draw stick figures without heads around the school house. Tape pennies at the top of each stick figure. Explain that during the year their minds will be filled with many wonderful things to think about. Each child traces around a penny with a felt pen to draw the missing head. Then they remove the penny to take home.

AUTUMN TREE

MATERIALS

Butcher paper, tape, felt pens, crayons.

PREPARATION

Secure a large sheet of butcher paper on a wall. Draw a large tree trunk on the paper and have the children color it with different shades of brown crayon.

LEARNING CIRCLE ACTIVITY

1. One child chooses a felt pen and draws an autumn leaf near the tree trunk. Give no limitations on size or shape!
2. Each child, in turn, draws a leaf and colors it with crayons.
3. Encourage the children to add leaves throughout the week.

MATERIALS FOR EXPANDING KNOWLEDGE

Felt, scissors, paper, pens, tape.

EXPANDING KNOWLEDGE

Cut out leaves from a variety of colors of felt. Print an Autumn Tree question on one side of each leaf and tape them onto the Autumn Tree. Have each child choose a felt leaf and answer the question. Suggested questions are:
If you were an autumn leaf, what color would you be?

What leaf on the Autumn Tree would you like to be? Why?
Would you feel scared if you were a leaf at the very top of a tree?
If you were a leaf and you fell on the ground, what could happen to you?
If you were a tree and someone was picking your prettiest leaves, what would you say to that person?
If you were a tree, what kind of animals could live in you?
Would you like to be an Autumn tree? Why?
If all your leaves fell to the ground, how would you feel?
What is a good name for our Autumn Tree?
If our Autumn Tree could hear, what would you say to it?

TEACHING TIPS

When a child pulls a leaf off the Autumn Tree to answer a leaf question have everyone say "ouch!" Encourage the idea of taking good care of trees and plants.

AUTUMN BREEZES

MATERIALS

Construction paper, scissors, feathers.

PREPARATION

Cut each sheet of paper in half.

LEARNING CIRCLE ACTIVITY

1. Call a Learning Circle to discuss Autumn Breezes.
2. Spark interest with questions such as:
   How does a breeze feel?
   How does the wind feel?
   If you were an autumn breeze, what would you like to push, lift, or blow against?
3. After the breeze discussion each child chooses a feather and a sheet of construction paper.
4. The children fold their papers in half.
5. They stand up, drop their feathers, and create a breeze by waving their papers. Who can keep the feather up?

MATERIALS FOR EXPANDING KNOWLEDGE

A leaf, a cotton ball, a balloon, a kleenex, a paper cup, paper, a fan.

EXPANDING KNOWLEDGE

Drop a variety of objects and observe how a gentle breeze effects each one. Drop a leaf, a cotton ball, a balloon, a kleenex, a paper cup, and a crunched up piece of paper. Which one falls the quickest? Use a fan to create a wind. Drop the same objects in front of the fan and watch what happens!

TEACHING TIPS

Tell the children that when they complete this activity they may choose one of the objects to take home with their folded papers. Then they can share this experience at home.

LEAF WALK

MATERIALS

Paper bags, felt pens.

PREPARATION

Write the name of each child on a bag.

LEARNING CIRCLE ACTIVITY

1. Take the class on a walk to collect autumn leaves.
2. After the walk hold a Learning Circle to study the leaves.
3. Notice the different shapes and colors.
4. Ask questions like:
   Why do autumn leaves turn color?
   How is autumn different from the other seasons?
   Is the earth becoming warmer or colder?
   Why do autumn leaves become crunchy?
   Why don't we see them during the Winter?
   Where do they go?

MATERIALS FOR EXPANDING KNOWLEDGE

White paper, crayons, tape, paint, paint-brushes, glue.

EXPANDING KNOWLEDGE

Make leaf prints. Place a leaf under a white paper and rub the surface with a crayon or use different crayons over the same leaf.

Make leaf paintings. Tape leaves onto white paper and paint over the leaves and paper. Remove the leaves. The shape of the leaves will remain.

Create autumn trees. The children glue their leaves on a large sheet of paper. They draw a tree trunk and then add leaves, branches, blossoms, and a bird nest to this picture.

MATERIALS FOR TEACHING TIPS

Autumn leaf, contact paper.

TEACHING TIPS

During the Learning Circle discussion display a beautiful autumn leaf pressed between clear contact paper. The child whose hand is raised and wants to talk can hold the leaf. This child can then hand the leaf to the next quiet volunteer.

AUTUMN BOOK

MATERIALS

White paper, crayons, felt pens, clear contact paper, yarn, hole punch, tape, paper bags.

PREPARATION

None

LEARNING CIRCLE ACTIVITY

1. Take the children outside to search for autumn things to go in the classroom's Autumn Book. Autumn things can be leaves, flowers, ferns, twigs, or small rocks.
2. Have them notice what the autumn day looks like.
3. While outside ask questions like:
   Is the sky blue or cloudy?
   Is the grass wet or dry?
   Is it chilly or warm?
4. Back in the classroom have each child draw a picture of what they have just observed. Write the children's names on each paper.
5. Cover both sides of the pictures with contact paper.
6. Choose an autumn object from each child's collection and cover these with contact paper.
7. Punch holes along the edge of all the autumn pictures and objects and tie them together with yarn to create a classroom Autumn Book.
8. Keep this book in the classroom throughout the year. The children will enjoy seeing their artwork and remembering that special autumn day.

EXPANDING KNOWLEDGE:

Make a classroom book for each season. It is an enjoyable way to compare seasonal objects and the different interpretations of each season.

TEACHING TIPS

Be enthusiastic about the children's artwork. Tell them that they might create books when they grow up! Show a book from the library and discuss the words "author" and "illustrator." When they finish this activity they will be illustrators, too!

RAIN BRAINSTORMS

MATERIALS

White posterboard, grey crayon, paper, scissors, felt pen, tape, silver glitter, glue.

PREPARATION

Color the posterboard grey. Cut out teardrop shapes from paper to make raindrops. Write a Rain Brainstorm question on one side. Suggested questions are:

Where does the rain come from?

How does the rain make you feel?

Why does the earth need rain?

Do animals need rain?

What do we mean by it is drizzling or it is pouring?

Can we drink the rain?

Can we drink ocean water?

What activities can you do in the rain?

Where does the rain go when it hits the ground?

What do you do on a rainy day when you are home?

Tape the raindrops question-side down on the posterboard. Glue silver glitter around the picture to create the glistening effect of rain.

LEARNING CIRCLE ACTIVITY

1. Each child, in turn, chooses a raindrop.
2. They answer the rain question on the back. The Learning Circle can answer, too.

MATERIALS FOR EXPANDING KNOWLEDGE

A glass, water, a plate, bowls, sponges.

EXPANDING KNOWLEDGE

Hold up a glass of water and pretend that this water is the ocean. Spill some of the water out onto a plate. Leave the plate out overnight and check it the next day. What happened?

Make rain! Each child gets a bowl of water and a sponge. Pretend that the bowl of water is the ocean. The children place their sponges on top of the water. This is a cloud close to the ocean. Each child picks up the sponge and squeezes it over the bowl. Rain!

TEACHING TIPS

To keep interest growing tell the children that after their Rain Brainstorm session they will make rain!

RAIN SOUP

MATERIALS

A large container such as a wagon or a plastic bin, water, bags, a long stick.

PREPARATION

Must be done after a rain shower.

LEARNING CIRCLE ACTIVITY

1. After a rainfall take the children outside on a rain walk to collect wet things.
2. Put these things in bags.
3. Have them smell the air. Notice that special rain scent from wet grass, leaves, dirt, and trees.
4. In the classroom pour water into the large container. Have each child place their rain objects into the water.
5. After each child does this, they can stir the rain soup with a long stick.

MATERIALS FOR EXPANDING KNOWLEDGE

Bowls, water, cotton balls, paper, feathers, marbles, leaves, rocks.

EXPANDING KNOWLEDGE

Discuss how rain changes the appearance of objects. Give each child a bowl of water and a variety of objects such as cotton balls, paper, feathers, marbles, leaves, and rocks. Have the children place the objects into the water and observe how their appearance changes. After a snowfall, make snow soup!

TEACHING TIPS

All the children are eager to share their treasures for the rain soup. Support every individual marvel at each discovery.

WINTER WIND

MATERIALS

Candles, matches, books, feathers.

PREPARATION

None

LEARNING CIRCLE ACTIVITY

1. Call a Learning Circle to talk about the wind.
2. Some questions to ask about the wind are:
    What is the wind?
    Where does the wind come from?
    Can we see the wind?
    When does the wind help us?
    When is the wind harmful?
    When the wind leaves, where does it go?
3. Have every child blow forcefully into the palm of their hand. Feel the wind!
4. Have every child blow out a candle. The wind can be very strong. It can blow over trees and telephone poles!
5. Have every child blow on a book with their hand on the other side of the book. The wind cannot go through the book.
6. Next, have every child blow on a feather. Imagine a bird soaring on the wind using its feathers.

MATERIALS FOR EXPANDING KNOWLEDGE

A hair dryer, a scarf, a sock, a marble, a paper cup.

EXPANDING KNOWLEDGE

Use a hair dryer to demonstrate the effect that wind has on different objects. Use it on a feather, a scarf, a sock, a marble, and a paper cup. Some objects will roll, some are lifted up in the air, some need a stronger wind to move them, and some bounce.

TEACHING TIPS

Keep the hair dryer in view during the Learning Circle and the anticipation will keep interest alive.

COLD TALK

MATERIALS

Ice cubes, bowls.

PREPARATION

Make ice cubes.

LEARNING CIRCLE ACTIVITY

1. Give each child a bowl with ice cubes in it.
2. Tell them that they may feel the ice while discussing the cold questions.
3. Feeling the sensation of cold will intensify the experience.
4. Suggested questions are:
   How do you feel when you are cold?
   What feels cold when you touch it?
   When you feel cold, what can you do to feel warm?
   What do animals do when they feel cold?
   Would you rather feel hot or cold?

EXPANDING KNOWLEDGE

Act out some cold imagination games. Imagine walking barefoot in the snow or building an imaginary snowman. Push the snow together and round it out. Lift the body sections. Hunt for berries to make the buttons. Stand back and admire the snowman. Go camping. Set up a tent. Unfold sleeping bags and climb in. Zip up. It's a cold night!

MATERIALS FOR TEACHING TIPS

A puppet such as a polar bear or penguin, mittens.

TEACHING TIPS

During the Cold Talk activity a cold weather puppet such as a polar bear or penguin can ask the questions.

Wear mittens and rub your hands briskly at the start of a new question. Have everyone rub their hands together until a volunteer is chosen to answer.

FLOWER GARDEN

MATERIALS

Blue construction paper, glue, paint, paint-brushes, yellow yarn, cotton balls, popcorn, tissue paper.

PREPARATION

Pop popcorn. Cut up tissue paper into small pieces.

LEARNING CIRCLE ACTIVITY

1. Every child paints flower stems on their paper.
2. Have the children glue popcorn or tissue paper at the top of each stem to make the flowers.
3. Make a sun by gluing yellow yarn in a circular pattern on the paper.
4. Make clouds by stretching cotton balls and gluing them on the paper.

EXPANDING KNOWLEDGE

Ask the children:
   What else besides popcorn and tissue
      paper could be used to create a flower?
   What is another way to make a sun?
   How could grass be added to the picture?
Imagination is the magic of learning!

MATERIALS FOR TEACHING TIPS

Flower pot, soil, seeds.

TEACHING TIPS

The promise of a real flower garden with many types of flowers will reinforce the learning experience and interest will blossom.

BUTTERFLY WALK

MATERIALS

Twigs, white paper, felt pens, scissors, glue.

PREPARATION

Draw the basic shape of a butterfly on a sheet of paper and display it on a wall.

LEARNING CIRCLE ACTIVITY

1. Take a walk outside and hunt for butterflies.
2. Have each child find a twig or stick upon which a butterfly might want to rest.
3. Each child carries the twig back to the classroom.
4. At the Learning Circle give each child a sheet of paper.
5. Have them draw a butterfly on the paper.
6. Encourage the use of different colored felt pens to create wing patterns.
7. Have the children cut out their butterflies and glue them on their twig.

MATERIALS FOR EXPANDING KNOWLEDGE

Pictures of butterflies and moths.

EXPANDING KNOWLEDGE

Show pictures of different butterflies and moths. Ask questions like:
What would it feel like to be a butterfly?
How does a butterfly see the world?
Do you think it remembers being a caterpillar?

TEACHING TIPS

When hunting butterfly twigs explain that butterflies are very gentle, shy creatures. Loud noises and sudden movements will scare them away.

To spark their interest, tell the children that at the end of the activity, they will make their very own pets to take home.

SPRING HUNT

MATERIALS

Paper bags, felt pen.

PREPARATION

Write each child's name on a paper bag.

LEARNING CIRCLE ACTIVITY

1. Take a Spring Hunt outside to observe and collect spring things. Suggested spring things are grass, clover, wild flowers, dandelions, rocks, leaves, twigs, or even a ladybug.
2. While the children are collecting have them take a deep breath to experience the smell of spring.
3. Have them smell the flowers and grass.
4. Notice how a spring day looks from the ground to the sky.
5. Lie down to observe the day from a different angle or crouch down to see it from the perspective of a small animal. The items that are placed in the bags can be taken home and shared.

EXPANDING KNOWLEDGE

Call a Learning Circle. Have each child share what he or she has collected. Discuss the various objects noting their color and texture. Imagine what the earth would be like without one of these items.

MATERIALS FOR TEACHING TIPS

Construction paper.

TEACHING TIPS

Everyone is eager to share their treasures, but waiting for a turn is difficult. As each child shows an item the other children can search in their own bags for a similar find.

Give each child a different colored sheet of construction paper to place their spring things on. This will help prevent the items from scattering.

SPRING MURAL

MATERIALS

Butcher paper, crayons, scissors, magazines, paper, paint, paintbrushes, tape. Suggested Spring items: paintings by the children, dried flowers, tree bark, branches, leaves, pictures of insects and baby animals, and even Easter eggs!

PREPARATION

Secure the butcher paper on a wall. Print the word *Spring* on the butcher paper.

LEARNING CIRCLE ACTIVITY

1. To create a Spring Mural attach spring objects and pictures to the butcher paper.
2. Have the children paint flowers, grass, and butterflies on the Mural.
3. Have them cut out magazine pictures relating to spring and add them to the Mural.
4. Encourage them to bring spring items from home to put on the Mural.

MATERIALS FOR EXPANDING KNOWLEDGE

Felt pens, sunflower seeds, glue.

EXPANDING KNOWLEDGE

Discuss each item on the Mural, its importance, and the reasons why it is related to Spring.

Add something new to the Mural. See who can find what it is—a ladybug drawn on a flower or sunflower seeds glued in a corner.

Play a guessing game. Describe an object on the Mural and see who can guess it correctly.

Create a Summer, Winter, and Fall Mural that suggests the unique feeling and mood of each season.

TEACHING TIPS

The degree to which the children become involved is influenced by the enthusiasm of the teacher. Greet each new item as though seeing it for the first time.

When discussing the various spring items use a question and answer format. What spring things that fly in the air can go on the Mural? Ask for raised hands.

SUN POWER

MATERIALS

Yellow posterboard, magazines, scissors, tape, a black felt pen.

PREPARATION

Draw a large sun on the posterboard.

LEARNING CIRCLE ACTIVITY

1. Display the picture of the sun.
2. Have the children cut out sun-related pictures and activities from the magazines and tape them inside the sun.

EXPANDING KNOWLEDGE

Discuss the activities that can be enjoyed in the sun. Can any be done in the rain? Why would it be difficult?

Discuss the effect the sun has on the earth. Take the class outside. Have everyone face the sun. Breath deeply! How does the sun make you feel?

MATERIALS FOR TEACHING TIPS

Black posterboard, scissors.

TEACHING TIPS

Make a large rain cloud from black posterboard. If the Learning Circle becomes too noisy or wiggly, cover the sun with the rain cloud. Explain that the sun does not like to hide. When everyone is quiet, the rain cloud will disappear!

SUMMER KITE

MATERIALS

Blue posterboard, a black felt pen, crepe paper, scissors, tape, magazines.

PREPARATION

Draw a large kite on the posterboard. With tape, secure a long streamer of crepe paper at the bottom on the kite. Select a magazine with pictures of summer activities in it.

LEARNING CIRCLE ACTIVITY

1. Show the magazine to the Learning Circle.
2. Stop at every picture that depicts an activity or idea enjoyed during the summer months.
3. Tear out each page after talking about it.
4. The children trim these pictures.
5. At the end of the discussion have each child choose a picture and tape it to the crepe paper streamer to make the kite tail.

MATERIALS FOR EXPANDING KNOWLEDGE

Twigs, yarn, butcher paper, scissors, a record or tape of ocean sounds.

EXPANDING KNOWLEDGE

Choose an activity from the kite tail and act it out. Go fishing! Give each child a twig with a piece of yarn tied to it. This is the fishing pole. Each child sits in a large Learning Circle and casts his or her pole into the circle. The teacher "swims" inside the circle and gently pulls on someone's yarn. This child says, "I caught something!" The teacher says, "What did you catch?" Enjoy the answers!

To become surfers, each child stands on a piece of butcher paper cut in the shape of a surfboard. They bend their knees and balance with their arms. Surf to music!

Swim across the classroom. Demonstrate various arm movements for the children to copy. Try the backstroke, frontstroke, sidestroke, and dog paddle while playing a tape of ocean sounds in the background.

TEACHER TIPS

In the Learning Circle the children can clap whenever they see a magazine page with a summer activity on it. This focuses thinking.

SUMMER BRAINSTORMS

MATERIALS

White posterboard, crayons, paper, felt pens, scissors, tape.

PREPARATION

Draw and color a dark cloud and a lightening bolt on the posterboard. Cut strips of paper and write a summer question on one side. Suggested questions are:

If you were an ice cream cone, what flavor would you be?

If you were a beach towel, what picture would be drawn on you?

Why would it be fun to be a fish in the ocean?

If you could go anywhere on a summer vacation, where would you go?

If you hiked to the very top of a mountain, what do you think you would see?

If you opened your eyes under the ocean, what do you think you would see?

Why would it be fun to be a kite?

If you were a popsicle, what color would you be?

If you went on a summer picnic, what would you bring to eat?

If you planted a summer garden, what would you plant?

Tape the strips of paper, question-side down, under the cloud like drops of rain. Draw a question mark on each paper strip using different colors to add visual stimulation.

LEARNING CIRCLE ACTIVITY

1. Have each child, in turn, choose a paper strip and answer the question written on the back.

EXPANDING KNOWLEDGE

To teach the children how to form questions, have each child make up a question to ask the Learning Circle. Guidance will be necessary in the beginning.

MATERIALS FOR TEACHING TIPS

Posterboard, scissors.

TEACHING TIPS

The child who is asking the question can hold a large question mark made from colored posterboard. This child can choose the next volunteer, who will hold the question mark.

SUMMER POSTERS

MATERIALS

Posterboards, felt pens, crayons, tape.

PREPARATION

Draw a summer object on each posterboard. Summer objects can be a sailboat, a flower, a beach ball, sunglasses, or a watermelon. Use many colors to draw and color each picture. Print the name of the object on each poster. Highlight the first letter.

LEARNING CIRCLE ACTIVITY

1. Choose one poster each day.
2. Have each child repeat this sentence and fill in the blank, "It is summer and I see a _____." If the boat poster was chosen, fill in the blank with a word that begins with the letter *B*.
3. Help the children think of *B* words by acting them out.
4. When the flower poster is used fill in the blank with words that begin with the letter *F*, and so on.

EXPANDING KNOWLEDGE

During the winter months display winter posters with related words. Repeat the sentence, "It is winter and I see a _____." Make Halloween posters and repeat "It is Halloween and I see a _____!"

TEACHING TIPS

At the end of each poster activity play a memory game. See who can remember a word that filled in the blank. Clap when a word is remembered! Remember, learning and fun mixed together create the magic of learning.

SUMMER SUN

MATERIALS

Yellow posterboard, felt pens, glue, yellow, red, and orange tissue paper, scissors.

PREPARATION

Draw a large sun on the posterboard. Cut up tissue paper into large pieces.

LEARNING CIRCLE ACTIVITY

1. Spread glue over the surface of the sun.
2. Each child crumples up a piece of tissue paper and presses it onto the sun.
3. As the children take their turn, they say this sentence and fill in the blank, "I am the sun and I warm _____!" An appreciation of the summer sun is encouraged.

MATERIALS FOR EXPANDING KNOWLEDGE

Globe, paper bags, flashlight.

EXPANDING KNOWLEDGE

Discuss the summer season. Explain that the earth is leaning more towards the sun, which is why the days are warmer. Show a globe of the earth and tilt it slightly towards the sun on the posterboard. Everyone can lean slightly towards the sun!

Take the class on a summer hunt to collect summer things for the Learning Circle. Darken the room and shine a flashlight on each object. Notice how the objects shimmer and gleam. Talk about the colors of summer and how sunshine makes everything look bright and alive.

TEACHING TIPS

Use the large rain cloud from the Sun Power activity. When the Learning Circle becomes too noisy, place the cloud over the Summer Sun. The sun likes to shine on a quiet Learning Circle. Help the sun to come out!

THE HELLO SONG

MATERIALS

White posterboard, scissors, felt pens, tape, magazines.

PREPARATION

Cut the posterboard into ten six-inch squares. Draw an animal or object on each square or tape a picture on each square. The pictures are a crocodile, a rainbow, a buttercup, a kangaroo, sunshine, a basset hound, a pelican, a manta ray, a panda bear, and a fly. Learn the Hello Song.

LEARNING CIRCLE ACTIVITY

1. Call a Learning Circle.
2. Chant this song whenever appropriate, for example, at the beginning of the year and whenever a new child enters the class.
3. Have everyone clap their hands slowly to establish a rhythm.
4. The teacher says each line, then everyone repeats the line.
5. Display each picture at the appropriate time in the song.
6. This song says hello ten different ways!

Stay awhile, Crocodile.
Say hello, Rainbow.
What's up, Buttercup?
How are you, Kangaroo?
Lookin' fine, Sunshine.
Stick around, Basset Hound.
Be a friend, Pelican.
Stay and play, Manta Ray.
Let's share, Panda Bear.
And hi, said the Fly!

EXPANDING KNOWLEDGE

Play a memory game! Say only the first part of each sentence. See who can remember the rhyming word at the end. Say the animal at the end of the line. See who can remember the different ways to say hello.

TEACHING TIPS

Pass out the picture cards in a different order than they are sung in the song. The children hold up their picture as it is sung.

BIRTHDAY CANDLE SONG

MATERIALS

None

PREPARATION

Learn the Birthday Candle Song.

LEARNING CIRCLE ACTIVITY

1. The children stand in a circle holding hands. They are the birthday candles.
2. The birthday child stands in the middle of the circle.
3. The children walk in a circle and sing the Birthday Candle Song to the tune of "Mary Had a Little Lamb."

   Time to sing our birthday song,
   Birthday song, birthday song.
   Time to sing our birthday song,
   As we go round and round.

   Make a wish and blow us down,
   Blow us down, blow us down.
   Make a wish and blow us down,
   As we go round and round.

4. After the children sing the last line, have the birthday child make a wish and blow around the circle.
5. The children who are candles fall down.

EXPANDING KNOWLEDGE

To make this a counting experience, the birthday child can count the "candles" on the cake. As this child counts, he or she taps the head of each child in the circle to "light the wick."

TEACHING TIPS

To prevent "candles" from falling wildly, suggest that they melt down to the ground.

THE GOODBYE SONG

MATERIALS

White posterboard, scissors, felt pens, tape, magazines.

PREPARATION

Cut the posterboard into ten six-inch squares. Draw or tape an animal picture on each square. The animals are an alligator, a butterfly, a ladybug, a parakeet, a jellyfish, a raccoon, a polar bear, a dinosaur, King Kong, and a fly. Learn the Goodbye Song.

LEARNING CIRCLE ACTIVITY

1. Call a Learning Circle.
2. Chant this song when appropriate, for example, when a child leaves the class. Chant this song on a Friday!
3. Have everyone clap their hands slowly to establish a rhythm.
4. The teacher says each line, then the children repeat each line.
5. Display the animal pictures on a wall or show them at the appropriate time in the song.
6. This song says goodbye ten different ways!

See you later, Alligator.
Bye bye, Butterfly.
Give a hug, Ladybug.
Be sweet, Parakeet.
Blow a kiss, Jellyfish.
See ya soon, Raccoon.
Take care, Polar Bear.
Out the door, Dinosaur.
So long, King Kong.
And bye, said the Fly!

EXPANDING KNOWLEDGE

Use this song to introduce words that rhyme. Play a rhyming activity. Ask each child, in turn, to name an animal or an object. If the word *dog* is named, say the words, "milk, grass, hog, and sun," repeating *dog* after each word. Help the children to recognize the two words that rhyme. Have them clap when they hear the words that rhyme.

TEACHING TIPS

Give each child an animal card to hold during the Goodbye Song. The children hold up their animal as it is sung.

AWARE OF ME SONG

MATERIALS

None

PREPARATION

Learn the "Aware of Me Song."

LEARNING CIRCLE ACTIVITY

1. Sing the Aware of Me Song to the tune of "There's a Spider on the Floor."
2. Follow the directions in the song.

Put your finger on your head, on your head,
Put your finger on your head, on your head,
Put your finger on your head, there's a dragon in your bed,
Put your finger on your head, on your head.

Put your finger on your ear, on your ear,
Put your finger on your ear, on your ear,
Put your finger on your ear, is a Stegasaurous near,
Put your finger on your ear, on your ear.

Put your finger on your nose, on your nose,
Put your finger on your nose, on your nose,
Put your finger on your nose, does an elephant have toes,
Put your finger on your nose, on your nose.

Put your finger on your cheek, on your cheek,
Put your finger on your cheek, on your cheek,
Put your finger on your cheek, and eat ice cream for a week,
Put your finger on your cheek, on your cheek.

Put your finger on your arm, on your arm,
Put your finger on your arm, on your arm,
Put your finger on your arm, would you buy a turkey farm,
Put your finger on your arm, on your arm.

Put your finger on your wrist, on your wrist,
Put your finger on your wrist, on your wrist,
Put your finger on your wrist, should a crocodile be kissed,
Put your finger on your wrist, on your wrist.

Put your finger on your tummy, on your tummy,
Put your finger on your tummy, on your tummy,
Put your finger on your tummy, do you think a frog is funny,
Put your finger on your tummy, on your tummy.

Put your finger on your thigh, on your thigh,
Put your finger on your thigh, on your thigh,
Put your finger on your thigh, would you eat a spider pie,
Put your finger on your thigh, on your thigh.

Put your finger on your knee, on your knee,
Put your finger on your knee, on your knee,
Put your finger on your knee, would a dinosaur eat me,
Put your finger on your knee, on your knee.

Put your finger on your toe, on your toe,
Put your finger on your toe, on your toe,
Put your finger on your toe, can you tell a gorilla no,
Put your finger on your toe, on your toe.

MATERIALS FOR EXPANDING KNOWLEDGE

Felt pens, white posterboard.

EXPANDING KNOWLEDGE

Draw an outline of a human body on posterboard. Add ears, eyes, mouth, and nose. Once this song is learned, one child can stand by the human body drawn on the posterboard. The child points to a part of the body mentioned in the song. If the thigh is selected first, sing the verse about the thigh. Sing the song in a different order.

MATERIALS FOR TEACHING TIPS

A doll or teddybear.

TEACHING TIPS

During this song sit a doll or large teddybear on your lap and point to its appropriate body parts.

THE TODAY SONG

MATERIALS

None

PREPARATION

Learn The Today Song.

LEARNING CIRCLE ACTIVITY

1. Sing The Today Song to the tune of "Skip To My Lou."
2. Follow the directions in the song.

Clap, clap, clap your hands,
Clap, clap, clap your hands,
Clap, clap, clap your hands,
Clap your hands today.

Blink, blink, blink your eyes,
Blink, blink, blink your eyes,
Blink, blink, blink your eyes,
Blink your eyes today.

Bend, bend, bend your thumb,
Bend, bend, bend your thumb,
Bend, bend, bend your thumb,
Bend your thumb today.

Pinch, pinch, pinch your ears,
Pinch, pinch, pinch your ears,
Pinch, pinch, pinch your ears,
Pinch your ears today.

Squeeze, squeeze, squeeze your knees,
Squeeze, squeeze, squeeze your knees,
Squeeze, squeeze, squeeze your knees,
Squeeze your knees today.

EXPANDING KNOWLEDGE

Talk about the different things that you can do with various parts of your body. What can you do with your hand? Shake it, squeeze it, rotate it, and wave it! Let each child choose a motion for a part of the body.

MATERIALS FOR TEACHING TIPS

A puppet.

TEACHING TIPS

Use a puppet to demonstrate the body movements. Have the good listeners in the Learning Circle use the puppet for one of the verses.

A SUMMER DAY SONG

MATERIALS

None

PREPARATION

Learn the song.

LEARNING CIRCLE ACTIVITY

1. Sing this song to the tune of "Do You Know The Muffin Man?"
2. Use finger movements to represent the different insects in the song. Make your fingers crawl slowly for a ladybug. Hook your thumbs together and wave your fingers for a butterfly. Pinch your thumb and first finger together for a honeybee. Wiggle your fingers close together for a firefly. Put your fingers together and place them on the floor. Move your hand upward and spread out your fingers for a hopping grasshopper.

Can you find a ladybug, a ladybug, a ladybug,
Can you find a ladybug who loves a Summer day?

Can you find a butterfly, a butterfly, a butterfly,
Can you find a butterfly who loves a Summer day?

Can you find a honeybee, a honeybee, a honeybee,
Can you find a honeybee who loves a Summer day?

Can you find a firefly, a firefly, a firefly,
Can you find a firefly who loves a Summer day?

Can you find a grasshopper, a grasshopper, a grasshopper,
Can you find a grasshopper who loves a Summer day?

EXPANDING KNOWLEDGE

Each child can think of an insect. Make up your own verses!

Sing this song using the names of animals common to the other seasons.

TEACHING TIPS

Tell the children that during this song their hands will turn into many insects! Encourage them to participate in the finger plays. Tell them that you hope you do not see any hands (just insects) in the Learning Circle.

MUSICAL PAINT

MATERIALS

White butcher paper, tape, paint, brushes, bowls, instrumental or recorded music.

PREPARATION

Secure a large sheet of butcher paper on the floor.

LEARNING CIRCLE ACTIVITY

1. Have the children sit around the butcher paper.
2. Place bowls of paint in the middle of the paper.
3. Play music or a record.
4. The children paint to the music. Encourage them to paint with their entire arm.

EXPANDING KNOWLEDGE

While the children are painting, stop the music. When the music starts again, the children change colors.

Using only two colors, paint two separate murals. Paint one to fast music and one to slow music. Is there a difference in the brush strokes?

Paint to different types of music. Paint to sounds like rain falling or thunder!

TEACHING TIPS

Ask the children not to speak while they are painting to music. This will help them to feel the mood that the music is creating. If the noise level begins to grow, signal a quiet sound.

MUSIC MOODS

MATERIALS

Instrumental or recorded music, playdough. Suggestions for music are ocean sounds, thunderstorm sounds, ballet, marching music, and lullabies.

PREPARATION

Make or purchase playdough. (A recipe can be found in Chapter Two.)

LEARNING CIRCLE ACTIVITY

1. Give each of the children a mound of playdough.
2. Discuss with the children that music can make them feel different ways.
3. Play music or a record.
4. The children shape the playdough according to the mood of the music.

EXPANDING KNOWLEDGE

The children close their eyes and listen to the music. Discuss how the music made them feel. What were they thinking about while they were listening?

TEACHING TIPS

During this activity space the children one or two feet away from each other to lessen distractions and increase concentration.

BALLOON STORIES

MATERIALS

Yellow, orange, blue, white, black, and gray balloons, a bell, instrumental or recorded music.

PREPARATION

Blow up the balloons. Learn the story.

LEARNING CIRCLE ACTIVITY

1. Give each child a balloon, distributing some of each color.
2. Have everyone sit in a corner of the classroom.
3. Play soft music. The children are going to dance out a story!
4. The teacher narrates the story. A suggested story: *The Rainstorm*. The teacher begins the story by saying, "It is morning. The sun is beginning to shine."
5. Have the children who are holding yellow and orange balloons dance to the middle of the room. Encourage them to move their balloons to the music.
6. After a minute ring a bell to signal the sun group to dance back to the corner.
7. "The sky is bright blue with only a few white clouds." Have the children who are holding the blue and white balloons dance into the room.
8. Ring the bell and these children move back to the corner.
9. "The nice weather does not last long. A storm is coming! Black clouds are filling the sky. Rain is starting to fall." Have the children holding the black and gray balloons begin to dance.
10. Ring the bell and these children move back to the corner.
11. "The storm is moving away. I can see the sun!" Have the yellow and orange balloon dancers move to the music.
12. "A few raindrops are still falling." The gray balloon dancers join in.
13. "A rainbow appears and makes a beautiful arch across the sky." Have all the balloon dancers join in!

EXPANDING KNOWLEDGE

Narrate different stories. When learning about Spring use green balloons for grass and red balloons for ladybugs. Have butterflies join in holding rainbow balloons. Use black and orange balloons for honeybees.

TEACHING TIPS

For very young children, first tell the story without the movements and then repeat it with movements. Ask for volunteers to ring the bell during the story. After a child has had a turn, he or she passes it on to another child. Adding an extra spark keeps interest alive.

HAND DANCING

MATERIALS

Instrumental or recorded music, hands!

PREPARATION

None

LEARNING CIRCLE ACTIVITY

1. Discuss different ways to move hands and fingers to music.
2. Play some music.
3. The children copy the teacher's hand movements. Suggested hand movements are: clapping hands, shaking hands, opening and closing fists, moving thumbs up and down, and moving fingers together and apart.

EXPANDING KNOWLEDGE

Lead the children in Hand Dancing and change the hand movement without giving a warning. See who can notice the new movement first!

The children can take turns leading the Learning Circle in Hand Dancing.

MATERIALS FOR TEACHING TIPS

Posterboard, felt pens, scissors, tape.

TEACHING TIPS

Draw a face on a posterboard. Draw two earplugs that fit the ears. Cut these out. Tape them on the posterboard near the face. When the Learning Circle becomes too noisy, tape the earplugs in the ears! Take them out when the Learning Circle is quiet.

POP GOES THE WEASEL

MATERIALS

White posterboard, scissors, broad-tip marker.

PREPARATION

Prepare large alphabet flashcards with the posterboard. Draw the letters with a broad-tip marker.

LEARNING CIRCLE ACTIVITY

1. Begin this game with five alphabet flashcards.
2. Choose a child to be the Weasel.
3. While everyone is singing the song "Pop Goes The Weasel," place the flashcards face down on the floor.
4. When the children sing the word "pop" in the song, the Weasel turns over one of the cards.
5. At the end of the song the Weasel identifies the letter and then chooses the next Weasel.
6. Add more letters to the group until everyone has had a turn. Review different letters each day, especially those that seem hard to recognize.

EXPANDING KNOWLEDGE

Make small flashcards. Play this activity with two sets of matching cards. On the word "pop" a child turns over two cards for a possible match. Use different colored felt pens to draw the letters. Use the same color to draw matching letters.

Display the children's names on separate wordstrips. On the word "pop" the Weasel tries to turn over a flashcard that has a letter from his or her name on it.

TEACHING TIPS

When a child is ready to choose the next Weasel, ask everyone to act like a Weasel. Have the children squint their eyes and sit very still. A wiggly Weasel will not be picked!

MR. HAPPY

MATERIALS

A box, white paper, felt pens, scissors.

PREPARATION

Decorate a Happy Face box. Draw happy faces on the sides. On separate pieces of paper draw happy face stick figures with their arms in different positions. Suggested positions are hands on head, hands on elbows, one arm raised and one arm on the waist, one hand touching the nose and one hand touching a knee, and both hands behind the back. Place these pictures in the box.

LEARNING CIRCLE ACTIVITY

1. Select a child with a happy face!
2. Have this child choose a picture from the Happy Face box.
3. Then this child stands in front of the Learning Circle and places his or her arms in the same position as Mr. Happy Face.

MATERIALS FOR EXPANDING KNOWLEDGE

Posterboard, white paper, felt pen, tape.

EXPANDING KNOWLEDGE

Prepare two matching sets of Mr. Happy Face cards. Display one set on a posterboard and leave one set in the box. One child chooses a card from the box and finds its twin on the posterboard. Now copy the arm position stretching minds and muscles!

MATERIALS FOR TEACHING TIPS

Posterboard, felt pen.

TEACHING TIPS

Display a picture of a large Mr. Happy Face. If attention slips, turn his happy face over to reveal a sad face. He does not like to feel sad! Let's make him happy again. When you have grabbed their attention, flip it back!

SCARF DANCING

MATERIALS

Scarfs, instrumental or recorded music.

PREPARATION

None

LEARNING CIRCLE ACTIVITY

1. Have each child choose a scarf.
2. Tell the children that the scarf is going to dance with them.
3. Play the music and have everyone move the scarfs to the music.
4. Talk about how different music might effect their movements.

EXPANDING KNOWLEDGE

Listen to the music and then turn it off. Have the children dance in silence. Encourage them to hear the music in their minds.

Use the scarfs to act out different ideas. Play music and dance like butterflies with shimmering wings. Be ocean waves or gentle breezes.

TEACHING TIPS

Increase interest in the activity by adding an extra incentive. Choose a child for each dance to hold two scarfs.

CLIP, CLAP, CLIP

MATERIALS

White posterboard, felt pens, tape, scissors.

PREPARATION

Prepare large alphabet flashcards on squares of posterboard. Tape each letter square on the wall with the letters face down. Learn the song Clip, Clap, Clip.

LEARNING CIRCLE ACTIVITY

1. Choose a Flipper.
2. Sing the Clip, Clap, Clip Song to the tune of "The Three Blind Mice."
3. Sing the last line in the same tune as the first line!

   Clip, Clap, Clip,
   Which one will you flip?
   Left or right, or high or low,
   By your head, or by your toe,
   Clip, Clap, Clip . . . . Flip!

4. When the last line is sung and everyone yells "flip", the Flipper chooses a letter square to flip over and identifies the letter.

EXPANDING KNOWLEDGE

Think of a word that begins with that letter. Focus on a specific category such as shapes, colors, or animals.

MATERIALS FOR TEACHING TIPS

Posterboard, scissors, felt pens, tape.

TEACHING TIPS

Make a small dolphin out of posterboard. Draw a swimming pool to fit the dolphin from the remaining posterboard. After identifying the letter, each child hands the dolphin to the next Flipper who places it back in the water. This will reinforce the concept of taking turns.

DINOSAUR STOMP

MATERIALS

A box, paper, scissors, felt pens.

PREPARATION

Cut paper into squares. Print a number from one to twenty on each of the squares and place these in a box. Learn the Dinosaur Stomp.

LEARNING CIRCLE ACTIVITY

1. Sit down and have everyone pound their fists on the floor in a slow, steady rhythm.
2. Chant the Dinosaur Stomp.

Dinosaur, dinosaur,
Can't catch me,
You're too slow and clumsy.
Stomping on a jungle tree,
Please don't ever stomp on me!

3. How many times did the Dinosaur stomp?
4. Have a child choose a number from the box.
5. If the number five is chosen, the child will answer, "five times!"
6. Have everyone pound their fists five times.

EXPANDING KNOWLEDGE

Say the Dinosaur Stomp and end the chant by pounding five times and saying "stomp" with each pound. What did the dinosaur stomp on? Repeat the chant and ask another child. Imagination is the greatest mind stretcher!

TEACHING TIPS

To prevent wild jungle pounding tell the children that if a dinosaur starts to run wild, it will fall into a dinosaur trap and will not be able to climb out. Then the game will have to end!

SHARK

MATERIALS

White posterboard, felt pens, scissors.

PREPARATION

Cut the posterboard into playing card shapes. On one card draw a shark. Print the word shark under the picture. On the remaining cards draw a picture of a fish. Print the word fish under each picture. Color the fish pictures different colors. Learn the Shark song.

LEARNING CIRCLE ACTIVITY

1. Sit in a circle and sing the Shark song to the tune of "Twinkle, Twinkle, Little Star."
2. While singing this song everyone moves their hands like fish swimming.

   I'm a fish as you can see,
   Swimming, swimming happily,
   Side to side and up and down,
   Diving deep to look around,
   Swimming, swimming, happily,
   Hope a shark does not eat me!

3. Choose a child to be the Shark.
4. Have this child walk around the inside of the Learning Circle and place a card, face down, in front of each child. Then the shark says "yum, yum," rubs his or her stomach, and everyone turns over their card. The child with the shark card collects all the fish cards and becomes the next Shark.

EXPANDING KNOWLEDGE

Introduce new words during the year. Use the words shark and eel or shark and clam, or use shark and seal to learn the letter *S*.

TEACHING TIPS

Remind the class that sudden movements attract sharks. Quiet fish have a better chance of not being caught!

ECHO RHYTHMS

MATERIALS

None

PREPARATION

Learn echo rhythms. Suggested echo rhythms are: clap once, wait, clap twice; clap three times quickly; clap twice, wait, clap twice; clap once, pound twice on the floor; and clap once, pound once, tap your stomach once.

LEARNING CIRCLE ACTIVITY

1. Start this activity by clapping once.
2. The children echo one clap.
3. Clap twice.
4. The children clap twice.
5. Clap three times. Try other rhythms. Who can echo the teacher's rhythm?

EXPANDING KNOWLEDGE

Have the children follow a series of verbal instructions touch your nose, your ear, and then your toes! Stand up, jump once, and turn around.

MATERIALS FOR TEACHING TIPS

Brown construction paper, scissors.

TEACHING TIPS

Promise that everyone will have a chance to create an echo for the class to follow. Each child, in turn, stands on a large square of brown construction paper. This is the top of a mountain and the child is a mountain climber. The mountain climber can make a noise or say a word and the Learning Circle echoes it.

BALLOON DANCING

MATERIALS

Balloons, instrumental or recorded music.

PREPARATION

Blow up the balloons.

LEARNING CIRCLE ACTIVITY

1. Give each child a balloon.
2. Play the music.
3. Encourage the children to dance with their balloons by holding them in their hands and moving with the rhythm of the music.

MATERIALS FOR EXPANDING KNOWLEDGE

Scarfs, crepe paper, feathers.

EXPANDING KNOWLEDGE

Dance with a variety of objects. Suggested objects are scarfs, crepe paper streamers, and feathers.

TEACHING TIPS

Tell the children that when their balloon dance is over, they can keep their balloons. This will encourage careful handling of the balloons.

THE ALPHABET GHOST

MATERIALS

White posterboard, scissors, broad-tip marker.

PREPARATION

Prepare large alphabet flashcards with the posterboard. Draw the letters with broad-tip markers. Learn the Alphabet Ghost Song.

LEARNING CIRCLE ACTIVITY

1. Begin with five flashcards face up on the floor.
2. Ask the children to study the letters.
3. After a short time turn the cards face down.
4. Choose a Ghost.
5. Have the Ghost take away one letter and hide it behind his or her back at the appropriate time in the song.

6. Sing the Alphabet Ghost Song to the tune of "Twinkle, Twinkle, Little Star."

   The ghost flies in right through the door
   And hunts for letters on the floor.
   He grabs them quick and hides them well.
   Where he hides them, he won't tell.
   Off he goes to wait some more
   For letters lying on the floor.

7. Turn the letters face up and see who can guess the missing letter.

EXPANDING KNOWLEDGE

Prepare wordstrips with ghost-related words printed on them. Display them on a white posterboard with the outline of a ghost around them. Place alphabet flashcards face up on the floor. Use only the letters that are in the ghost words. Choose a ghost writer! The ghost writer chooses a wordstrip and spells the word on the floor using the flashcards. The other children can act out the ghost word. If the word is boo, everyone yells "boo!" If the word is float, everyone floats around the Learning Circle. Other ghost words could be creep, scare, fly, and haunt.

Play this activity at other times such as during Thanksgiving or at Easter.

MATERIALS FOR TEACHING TIPS

Black posterboard, a tissue, string, tape.

TEACHING TIPS

Make a ghost from a tissue and hang it from a black posterboard. The child who is the Alphabet Ghost can make the ghost fly by giving it a good swing. The next Alphabet Ghost can make the ghost fly!

OVER, UNDER, AROUND, AND POUND

MATERIALS

White construction paper, a table, felt pens, scissors, tape.

PREPARATION

Prepare wordstrips with the words *Over, Under, Around,* and *Pound* printed on them. Print identical words in the same color. Tape the wordstrips on a wall face down. Print the letters *O, U, A* and *P* on a sign. Learn the song and movements. Move a table near the Learning Circle.

LEARNING CIRCLE ACTIVITY

1. Sing the song Over, Under, Around, and Pound to the tune of "London Bridges."

   Over, under, around and pound,
   Around and pound, around and
   *   pound,*
   O and U and A and P,
   Each has a different sound.

2. While singing this song, use hand movements to act out the words *Over, Under, Around,* and *Pound.*
3. For the word *Over,* keep the left hand straight and move the right hand over it.
4. For *Under,* keep the left hand in the same position and move the right hand under it.

5. For *Around,* move the right hand in a large circle.
6. For *Pound,* end the motion with a pound on the floor. Move smoothly from one motion to the next.
7. When singing the letters *O, U, A,* and *P,* point to these letters on the nearby sign.
8. After the song choose a child to pick a wordstrip from the wall.
9. Turn it over and stress the first letter of the word, then say the whole word.
10. If the word is *Over,* the child will go Over the table. The other choices will be going *Under* the table, walking *Around* the table, or *Pounding* on the table. After a few turns the children will begin to recognize what the word says.

EXPANDING KNOWLEDGE

Use different action words to cover many sounds such as Hop, Skip, Jump, and Dance.

TEACHING TIPS

Hide a surprise word among the wordstrips. Who will choose it! A hint of mystery and anticipation will keep interest alive. A good surprise word is *Slide. Slide* down the table!

MUSIC BOX

MATERIALS

A box, white construction paper, tape, felt pens, paper, scissors, instrumental or recorded music.

PREPARATION

Decorate a box. Line the sides with construction paper. Draw musical notes on the sides using different colored felt pens. This is the Music Box. Prepare strips of paper with a moving-to-music activity written on it. Suggested movement ideas are ice-skating, birds flying, balancing on a ball, painting a large wall, walking in honey, driving a car on a winding road, rowing a boat, or riding a surfboard. Place these in the Music Box.

LEARNING CIRCLE ACTIVITY

1. Have a child choose a strip of paper from the Music Box.
2. Read the moving-to-music activity.
3. Then the child acts out the activity with instrumental or recorded music.

MATERIALS FOR EXPANDING KNOWLEDGE

A selection of instrumental or recorded music.

EXPANDING KNOWLEDGE

Move to different types of music such as classical, ballet, jazz, soft rock, and western.

Play a variety of records where the main instrument is different. The children can pretend they are playing a piano, drums, a violin, or a harp. Discuss the different body movements for each instrument.

MATERIALS FOR TEACHING TIPS

A bell, a can of beans, or a tambourine.

TEACHING TIPS

Provide a special sound that will tell the children when to end a movement activity. Ring a bell, shake a can of beans, or shake a tambourine.

THE CHICKEN AND THE FOX

MATERIALS

None

PREPARATION

None

LEARNING CIRCLE ACTIVITY

1. Choose a child to be the Fox. The rest of the children are the Chickens.
2. Whisper a different color in the ear of every Chicken. That is the color of his or her "eggs."
3. The Fox tries to guess the colors that were given to each of the Chickens.
4. When the Fox guesses the correct color of a Chicken's "egg," the Chicken squawks and moves back a foot from the Learning Circle. The Chicken leaves its nest to give the Fox its "egg!"
5. The last Chicken to move off its nest is the next Fox.

EXPANDING KNOWLEDGE

Instead of colors whisper zoo animal names, shapes, or ice cream flavors.

TEACHING TIPS

Tell the children that a quiet place is needed for a group of Chickens sitting on their eggs!

THE SAME GAME

MATERIALS

White posterboard, felt pens, pennies.

PREPARATION

Draw the Same Game on white posterboard. Draw horizontal and vertical lines to make squares, approximately three inches by three inches, on the board. Draw round faces inside each square. Each face will have two eyes and a mouth. Each face will have an identical twin somewhere on the game board. Suggested faces are a happy face, a sad face, a mad face, a scared face, a sleepy face, a winking face, or a pirate face with a patch.

LEARNING CIRCLE ACTIVITY

1. Have the children look at the board while the teacher talks about the different faces.
2. Place the board on the floor.
3. Give each child two pennies.
4. Have each child, in turn, try to toss their pennies on two faces that are identical.

EXPANDING KNOWLEDGE

Draw the matching faces with the same color felt pen. Print names by each face. Draw a Mr. Silly, a Mrs. Happy, a Mrs. Winky, and a Mr. Mad! Draw a Mr. Tease with a tongue sticking out and a Mrs. Bubbles with a bubble over her mouth from chewing bubble gum! Ask the children for suggestions. Name all the different faces. See who can remember the names for each expression. When a name is remembered correctly, act it out!

Play this game with identical ladybugs. Use matching colors and spots. Try to match Easter egg designs at Easter!

TEACHING TIPS

Tell the Learning Circle that if they sit quietly, they may keep their pennies. If they keep their pennies for the whole game, they can take them home.

LADYBUG RACE

MATERIALS

White posterboard, red posterboard, large die, felt pens, scissors.

PREPARATION

Draw the boardgame on the white posterboard. Draw vertical lines two inches apart down the board and horizontal lines two inches apart across the board. In the last squares down the right side of the board draw houses. Print special messages in some of the squares. Suggested messages are fly ahead three spaces, crawl back one space, or fly home!

Prepare ladybug markers, one for each child, by cutting circles from the red poster-board. Draw eyes and spots on each one. Place each ladybug on the first row of squares going down. Print a child's name on each of the ladybug markers. Use the remaining red posterboard to label the left side *Start* and the right side *Home*.

LEARNING CIRCLE ACTIVITY

1. Have each child, in turn, roll the die and move his or her ladybug marker horizontally for the number of spaces on the die. Each child moves the ladybug marker with his or her name on it.
2. Continue until all of the ladybugs arrive home.
3. When each ladybug arrives home, the whole Learning Circle applauds. Everyone feels like a winner!

MATERIALS FOR EXPANDING KNOWLEDGE

Posterboard, felt pens.

EXPANDING KNOWLEDGE

Play this game when the class is learning about insects. Discuss the ladybug! Play this game at Easter with Easter bunnies moving towards their egg baskets. Play this game when someone is moving and is leaving the class. Use happy face markers to represent the child moving toward a new home.

TEACHING TIPS

Encourage minds to focus on the activity by having everyone count aloud the spaces that each ladybug moves.

MR. MOUSE

MATERIALS

White posterboard, yellow posterboard, felt pens, scissors, tape.

PREPARATION

Draw a large house on the white posterboard. Draw four vertical lines across the house to make it a four story house. Draw a total of twenty arches on the vertical lines for the mouse holes. Number the mouse holes. Cut out twenty mice from the remaining posterboard. Number the mice. Cut out pieces of cheese from the yellow posterboard.

LEARNING CIRCLE ACTIVITY

1. Have one child choose a mouse.
2. If the mouse's number is five, the child places the mouse in hole number five.
3. Then the child chooses a piece of cheese to feed the mouse and leaves the cheese in the mouse hole.
4. Repeat with another child until all the mice are home.
5. When all the mice have been placed in their mouse holes, they are safe from any hungry cats!

EXPANDING KNOWLEDGE

Discuss the concept of *Small*. Have each child finish the sentence, "If I was as small as a mouse, I could _____!" (fit in a shoe, sleep on a leaf.)

TEACHING TIPS

When a mouse is placed in a mouse hole, have everyone bend their fingers like claws and yell "meow!"

MRS. ELEPHANT

MATERIALS

White posterboard, felt pens, scissors, recorded or instrumental music.

PREPARATION

Draw twenty circles on the posterboard with a different shape inside each one. Suggested shapes are a circle, square, triangle, rectangle, half moon, star, heart, oval, octagon, cylinder, clover, diamond, or a design. These designs can be a flower shape, a bow tie, a fish, or a sun. These twenty circles are the circus rings.

Draw and cut out elephants from the remaining posterboard. Draw a blanket on each circus elephant with a different shape on each blanket, matching the shapes in the circus rings. Place the circus ring posterboard and the elephants on the floor in the middle of the Learning Circle.

LEARNING CIRCLE ACTIVITY

1. Have a child choose an elephant.
2. This child places it in the circus ring that has the same shape as the one on the elephant's blanket.
3. Repeat with another child until all the elephants have been placed in their rings.
4. Now the circus is ready to begin! Play some lively music and have the children walk and sway like elephants.

EXPANDING KNOWLEDGE

Discuss the concept of *Big*. Have each child finish the sentence, "If I was as big as an elephant, I could _____!" (touch the top of a tree, eat 100 pancakes.)

MATERIALS FOR TEACHING TIPS

Shelled peanuts, paper bags.

TEACHING TIPS

As each child places an elephant in its ring, have everyone clap like a circus audience! Place shelled peanuts in a small paper bag. After the children have placed their circus elephants in the rings, they can pick a peanut from the bag.

MYSTERY BOX

MATERIALS

A box, felt pens, the mystery object such as a stuffed animal, balloons, a bag of marshmallows, or a new toy for the classroom.

PREPARATION

Place a mystery object inside the box. Draw question marks on the sides of the box.

LEARNING CIRCLE ACTIVITY

1. Discuss what a question is. Explain the difference between a question and a statement. Give examples of both "The box is pretty." "What is in the box?" Which is the question?
2. Display the mystery box.
3. Have each child ask a question concerning the object that is hidden inside.
4. When everyone has had a turn, review the answers.
5. Give everyone a chance to make a guess.
6. The child who makes the correct guess can open the box and reveal the mystery object.

EXPANDING KNOWLEDGE

Try different versions of this activity. Show one child what is hidden in the box. Have this child answer the questions.

Have the children bring objects from home to hide in the mystery box. If the class is learning about the color blue, hide a blue object! Or if the topic is the ocean, place an ocean-related object in the box.

MATERIALS FOR TEACHING TIPS

Posterboard, felt pen, scissors.

TEACHING TIPS

Make a large question mark from posterboard. The child who is asking a question can hold the question mark. Have this child pass the question mark to the child who asks the next question.

BANKER

MATERIALS

A box, coins, posterboard, scissors, tape, felt pens.

PREPARATION

Cut a slit at the top of a box. This is the bank. Cut a large square from a posterboard. Tape on a penny, a nickel, a dime, and a quarter. Print the name of each coin underneath it.

LEARNING CIRCLE ACTIVITY

1. Display a selection of coins.
2. Select a Banker.
3. The Banker chooses a coin and finds the identical coin on the posterboard.
4. The Banker identifies the coin and drops it into the bank.

EXPANDING KNOWLEDGE

At the end of each week empty the bank and display the coins in the middle of the Learning Circle. Separate the different coins and group identical coins together. Count how much money was in the bank.

TEACHING TIPS

Promise a Banker party with the money that is saved. Offer a popcorn party, a sticker party, or a balloon party! Ask the children for party suggestions.

COLOR SLAP

MATERIALS

Colored construction paper, a black felt pen, scissors, a box.

PREPARATION

Cut out playing card shapes from different colored construction paper. Draw a heart on one of the cards. Draw an X on one side of every other card.

LEARNING CIRCLE ACTIVITY

1. Shuffle the cards.
2. Pass out six cards to each child, X-side down.
3. Have everyone put them in a straight line.
4. Put the remainder of the cards in a box.
5. The teacher chooses a card from the box.
6. If it is purple, say "purple" and show the card.
7. Everyone who has a purple card slaps it and turns it over.
8. If someone has two purple cards, only one card can be turned over.
9. Put the purple card back in the box and choose another card.
10. Continue drawing cards from the box until everyone has all their cards turned over. The child who turns over the heart card from the row of cards in front of them can choose the cards for the next game.

MATERIALS FOR EXPANDING KNOWLEDGE

Pennies.

EXPANDING KNOWLEDGE

Play this activity with shapes, numbers, or letters.

Play the game like Bingo. Give each child six pennies. Have the children place a penny on a matching color card.

TEACHING TIPS

Tell the children who have finished the game early that they can create designs on the floor with their color cards.

SPONGE EATER

MATERIALS

White posterboard, white paper, felt pens, sponges, scissors, two boxes.

PREPARATION

Draw and color a large monster on the posterboard. Cut out a large hole in the middle of the poster for the mouth. This monster eats sponges! Print numbers from one to ten on a sheet of paper. Cut them out and put them in a box. Cut up sponges into ten squares and put them in another box.

LEARNING CIRCLE ACTIVITY

1. Select a Sponge Thrower.
2. Have the Sponge Thrower choose a number from the box.
3. If the number is a three, have this child take three sponges from the other box and throw them into the mouth of the Sponge Eater.
4. Repeat until everyone has had a turn.

MATERIALS FOR EXPANDING KNOWLEDGE

Bubbles, paper, felt pens, scissors.

EXPANDING KNOWLEDGE

Begin by placing the Sponge Eater near the Sponge Throwers and then gradually increase the distance.

Make a Bubble Eater and blow bubbles into its mouth! Make a Letter Eater and a Color Eater. Make a Name Eater! Have the children print their names on paper, crumple them up, and throw them into the Name Eater's mouth.

TEACHING TIPS

The Sponge Eater gets very nervous around crowds and might refuse to eat! If everyone sits down in the Learning Circle and waits for a turn, then we will all have a chance to feed the monster.

MAKE A MONSTER

MATERIALS

White butcher paper, white paper, felt pens, scissors, tape, large die.

PREPARATION

Secure a large sheet of butcher paper on a wall. Draw a large outline of a head. Prepare wordstrips with the white paper. Print the name of a body part on one side. Tape these, word-side down, near the butcher paper.

LEARNING CIRCLE ACTIVITY

1. Choose the Monster Maker!
2. Have this child roll the die and choose a wordstrip.
3. If the number five was rolled and the word "eye" was chosen, the child can choose a felt pen and draw five eyes on the face.
4. Repeat until everyone has had a turn. If the class is large, add more body parts such as freckles, eyelashes, eyebrows, teeth, mouths, and navels so everyone can have a turn.

EXPANDING KNOWLEDGE

Talk about the body parts that are drawn on the monster. Ask questions like:

What would it be like to have five eyes?
What could you do if you had three legs?
If you had four arms, what could you do? (Hold four ice cream cones at the same time!)
Where do you think the monster came from?
What would you name the monster?

MATERIALS FOR TEACHING TIPS

A box of marbles.

TEACHING TIPS

After the Monster Maker completes a turn, he or she walks around the Learning Circle shaking a box of marbles. The monster is growling and is impatient for the rest of his body! When the marbles stop over someone's head, the next Monster Maker is chosen. The sound of the marbles is a great attention-grabber.

MISTER Q

MATERIALS

None

PREPARATION

None

LEARNING CIRCLE ACTIVITY

1. The Q in this activity stands for *Quiet*! When the Learning Circle looks more like a tank of worms than a circle of children, play Mister Q.
2. Tell the children that they will have one minute to perform an activity.
3. They can perform these activities fast or slow, as long as they stop at the special signal (see below).
4. Suggested Mister Q activities are scratching on the rug, hissing like wild snakes, shaking their hands, pounding fists on the rug, or slapping their knees.

EXPANDING KNOWLEDGE

Play Follow Mister Q! Have one child lead the class in Mister Q activities. When playing this activity, ask who can remember what the Q stands for. This is a good reminder of a hard letter sound.

TEACHING TIPS

The special signal is an important control technique. Make it very visible! Suggested signals are crossing arms high in the air and moving them apart, opening and closing fists in rapid motion, clapping hands loudly, snapping fingers, and tracing a large Q in the air using one finger. Use this special signal throughout the year whenever the Learning Circle needs a quiet reminder.

TRAVEL CORNER

MATERIALS

Posterboard, chairs, a box, felt pens, magazines, tape.

PREPARATION

Arrange chairs to resemble the seating on a train, an airplane, or a boat. Draw a control panel on the posterboard. Secure it on a wall. Make tickets from posterboard and place them in a box. Hang magazine pictures of places that are fun to visit.

LEARNING CIRCLE ACTIVITY

1. The children sit in the arranged chairs ready for an imaginary trip.
2. Decide whether everyone is traveling in a train, an airplane, or a boat and take off!
3. Have each child name an imaginary object that they can see while looking out of their imaginary windows.
4. After the trip is over, sit in a Learning Circle. See who can remember the objects that were seen on the trip.

EXPANDING KNOWLEDGE

Offer the Travel Corner for creative play experiences. Invite the children to take imaginary trips throughout the day. Watch imaginations take off! Visits to various planets can be encouraged when learning about space. Pictures of dinosaurs may mean a trip back to prehistoric time. During the Christmas holidays visit the North Pole. If a child is moving to a different state, visit the new location.

TEACHING TIPS

Encourage traveling in an orderly manner. Establish travel rules quiet passengers, one attendant, one captain, one ticket collector, and no stowaways!

NAME DESIGN

MATERIALS

Butcher paper, felt pens, tape.

PREPARATION

Secure a large sheet of butcher paper on a wall. Draw a large happy face on the paper. Print the names of the children on this paper.

LEARNING CIRCLE ACTIVITY

1. Use this happy face as a giant sign-in sheet.
2. Have each child at the Learning Circle choose a felt pen and print his or her name on the happy face.

EXPANDING KNOWLEDGE

Encourage the children to print their names any time during the day. Change the design of the sign-in sheet often. Draw a whale for a sign-in sheet when learning about sea-life. Draw a ghost at Halloween! Have everyone print the word *Boo*. Draw a turkey at Thanksgiving and print the word *Yum*.

MATERIALS FOR TEACHING TIPS

Happy face stickers.

TEACHING TIPS

Have everyone place a happy face sticker by their name after they have printed their name on the sheet.

BEE STING

MATERIALS

Orange posterboard, a black felt pen, scissors, paper cups.

PREPARATION

Cut the posterboard into squares. Print the letter *B* on some of the squares and the letter *E* on some of the squares. Place three squares in each paper cup to spell the word *Bee*.

LEARNING CIRCLE ACTIVITY

1. Give each child a paper cup with the squares in it to spell the word Bee.
2. Choose a child to be the Bee.
3. Have the children put their hand over the paper cup and shake it.
4. Have the Bee walk around the Learning Circle and "sting" someone by touching them on the back.
5. The child who was "stung" will yell "ouch!"
6. That is the signal for everyone to shake their letters on the floor and place them in the correct order to spell *Bee*.
7. When a child spells the word *Bee* he or she yells "sting!"
8. The child who was "stung" is the next Bee.

MATERIALS FOR EXPANDING KNOWLEDGE

Posterboard, felt pens, scissors.

EXPANDING KNOWLEDGE

Spell out other words such as moo, boo, dog, and cat. When the cat touches someone on the back, yell "squeak!". Make up other variations.

MATERIALS FOR TEACHING TIPS

Bee stickers, wire bees.

TEACHING TIPS

After the game is over, give a gift to each child to take home. Suggested ideas are bee stickers, wire bees found in craft stores, or the paper cups with the *Bee* word inside. Sending a part of the activity home helps the child to remember the game and to verbalize the experience at home.

CIRCUS TRAIN

MATERIALS

White butcher paper, felt pens, tape.

PREPARATION

Make a simple drawing of a circus train using squares for box cars and circles for wheels. Draw this on the butcher paper. Draw twenty-six box cars. Print an alphabet letter on each car. Attach the paper to a wall.

LEARNING CIRCLE ACTIVITY

1. The children in the Learning Circle are the animal buyers. They are in charge of filling the circus train with animals.
2. Have one child name an animal that they would like to put on the circus train.
3. If a child says a lion, the child must find the car that has the letter *L* printed on it.
4. Have the child choose a felt pen and draw two eyes and a smile above the car.
5. Print the name of the animal on the car.
6. Repeat with another child until everyone has had a turn or the train is full.

EXPANDING KNOWLEDGE

Use this activity as a memory game. See who can remember what animal was ordered for each letter.

Play animal charades! Choose a car and act out an animal from that car.

TEACHING TIPS

Tell the children that at the end of the activity they will all take a train ride. Tell the children to form a line and sit in their "box cars." You are the train conductor. As you take a "ticket" from each child, ask them what kind of animal they are. Now you are ready to go! Pull the train whistle and have everyone yell "Choo-choo!"

FISH TANK

MATERIALS

White posterboard, white construction paper, felt pens, crayons, scissors, tape.

PREPARATION

Draw a line three inches in from the edge around the posterboard. This is the fish tank. Draw a school of fish inside the fish tank. Print the first letter of a color word on each fish. Cut and color matching fish shapes from the white paper. Print the name of a color on each fish. Tape the fish around the outside of the tank in the three inch space. Color this outside space blue.

LEARNING CIRCLE ACTIVITY

1. Choose the Fish Finder.
2. Have this child choose a fish on the outside of the tank.
3. Have him or her identify the color of the fish.
4. Read the color word on the fish.
5. Have the Fish Finder say the first letter of this color word. If it is green, he or she tapes the green fish over the fish in the fish tank that has the letter *G* on it.
6. Continue until all the fish have jumped back into the tank.

MATERIALS FOR EXPANDING KNOWLEDGE

White posterboard, scissors, crayons, tape.

EXPANDING KNOWLEDGE

Introduce color words that are less common such as gold, silver, peach, violet, rust, and tan.

Give each child a colored circle cut from white posterboard. These circles are colored to match the fish. They are matching bubbles! Have each child find the matching fish and tape its bubble next to it. Let each child name the color of the matching fish.

TEACHING TIPS

Everyone will have a turn to put a fish back in the water. But fish lose their color when they are scared! We need to sit quietly so we can give the colors back to the fish.

FUNNY BONES

MATERIALS

White posterboard, felt pens, tape, white construction paper, scissors.

PREPARATION

Draw a human body on the posterboard. Cut squares from the paper and draw a picture of a body part on each square. Display the posterboard on a wall. Tape the body pictures face-down near the posterboard.

LEARNING CIRCLE ACTIVITY

1. Select a Doctor.
2. Have the Doctor choose a body part and show it to the Learning Circle.
3. If the body part is a chin, the children say, "Help, I hurt my chin!"
4. The Doctor will then tape the body picture over the same body part on the poster.
5. Continue until the body is complete and everyone has had a turn picking a body part.

EXPANDING KNOWLEDGE

Print the word, along with the body part, on the square of paper. The children in the Learning Circle point to their body part that is on the picture.

Each child chooses two body pictures. Can everyone touch both body parts at the same time?

MATERIALS FOR TEACHING TIPS

Red felt, scissors.

TEACHING TIPS

Cut out a heart shape from red felt. The Doctor hands the felt heart to the next Doctor who has been waiting quietly in the "waiting room."

FRECKLE FRED

MATERIALS

White butcher paper, felt pens, a box, paper, scissors, tape.

PREPARATION

Make a freckle box. Decorate a box with large freckles in many colors. Cut out paper strips with the numbers one to twenty printed on them and place them in the box. Draw a large face on the butcher paper. Attach to a wall.

LEARNING CIRCLE ACTIVITY

1. One child is selected to be the Freckle Finder.
2. Have the Freckle Finder choose a number from the box.
3. If the number five is chosen, the Freckle Finder chooses a felt pen and draws five freckles on Fred's face. Have the children draw small circle shapes for the freckles.
4. Continue until Freckle Fred's face is filled with freckles and everyone has had a turn.

MATERIALS FOR EXPANDING KNOWLEDGE

White butcher paper, felt pens.

EXPANDING KNOWLEDGE

When everyone has drawn their freckles, count the number of freckles! Invite the children to color the freckles. Instead of a face use a ladybug or a dalmation. Try a pizza and add the pepperoni. Add the spots on a giraffe!

TEACHING TIPS

To help the children anticipate the end result of the activity say, "Wait until you see how great Fred will look with rainbow freckles!"

MENU MUNCHIES

MATERIALS

Posterboard, felt pens, scissors, a tray, play food items such as small milk cartons, fruit cans, plastic utensils, napkins, plastic ketchup and mustard bottles, and plastic play food—hot dogs, cheese, beef, vegetables, apples, and bananas.

PREPARATION

Cut the posterboard into squares, approximately five inches by five inches. Draw from one to five food items on each square. Have the food items match the play food. These are the menu cards.

LEARNING CIRCLE ACTIVITY

1. Choose a child to be the Chef.
2. Ask for volunteers who have the munchies! Choose a Customer.
3. Have the Customer choose a menu card and hand it to the Chef.
4. The Chef fills the tray with play food that matches the pictures on the card and serves the Customer.

MATERIALS FOR EXPANDING KNOWLEDGE

Toy animals, a dish, pennies.

EXPANDING KNOWLEDGE

Match animal pictures! Choose a Customer and a Pet Store Owner. Have the Customer hand the Store Owner a picture of an animal to purchase. The Store Owner can hand the Customer a small play animal that matches the picture. Have a dish of pennies available. The Store Owner can ask for payment from one to ten pennies. As counting skills increase, offer twenty pennies.

MATERIALS FOR TEACHING TIPS

An apron, a Chef's hat.

TEACHING TIPS

The child who is the Chef gets to wear an apron or a Chef's hat. The ability to match identical items and increase perception skills go hand in hand with the fun.

BUILD A BURGER

MATERIALS

Construction paper, a black felt pen, scissors.

PREPARATION

Cut out circles and squares from different colored construction paper. These represent food items in a hamburger. Suggested food items are buns - brown circles, beef - pink circles, tomatoes - red circles, onion - white circles, pickles -dark green circles, lettuce -light green squares, cheese - orange squares, and mustard - yellow squares. Make one of each food item for each child in the class.

Cut out colored squares that match the colors of the food items. Print the first sound of the name of each food item on the squares. If cheese is orange, print the letters *Ch* on an orange square.

LEARNING CIRCLE ACTIVITY

1. Pass out the food items to everyone in the Learning Circle.
2. Place the colored letter cards on the floor.
3. Hold up a card such as the *M* card.
4. What goes on a hamburger that starts with an *M* sound? Guide the children towards the right answer. Pretend to squeeze a mustard bottle over a hamburger bun. Make the *M* sound while squeezing.
5. Proceed with each letter card until the burgers are built.

EXPANDING KNOWLEDGE

The children can decide what food item to put on next. They look for the letter card that shows the appropriate sound of their chosen food item. Build a different burger every time. Think of a name for the hamburger. What part of a hamburger is your favorite?

Don't stop with a hamburger! Try this activity with the parts of a snowman, a teddybear, or the toppings on a pizza.

TEACHING TIPS

Tell the children that after the activity, they can play Cook and Customer with the hamburger items.

Cover the food items with contact paper and they will survive many cooking games!

CRAZY FRUITS

MATERIALS

Colored construction paper, felt pens, scissors.

PREPARATION

Draw and cut out a variey of fruit from construction paper. Match the color of the fruit with the appropriate color of construction paper. Print the name of each fruit on a wordstrip, also matching colors. Make a red wordstrip for *apple* if a red *apple* was made. Cut the fruit words between each syllable, for example, for the word *apple* there will be two red strips. One will have the letters *ap* and the other will have *ple*. Place the fruit pictures on the floor inside the Learning Circle. Place the syllables on the floor near the fruit.

LEARNING CIRCLE ACTIVITY

1. Choose a Fruit Finder.
2. Have this child choose a fruit and identify it.
3. Then the child finds the colored syllable strips that match the fruit.
4. Help the child put the strips in the right order to spell the name of the fruit.
5. Say the name of the fruit.
6. Discuss the letter sound that the fruit begins with. Say the word slowly.

7. Listen for the letter sounds in the word.
8. Now it is time to make the crazy fruit! If *banana* was chosen, explain that these letters only spell the word *banana* if they are placed in a certain order.
9. Have the Fruit finder mix up the strips.
10. Read the word to the class. *na na ba*! If the Learning Circle is having fun, that is the magic of learning.

EXPANDING KNOWLEDGE

Play crazy animals or crazy insects. Play this game with everyone's first name!

MATERIALS FOR TEACHING TIPS

Green posterboard, scissors, felt pens.

TEACHING TIPS

Make a large green grape from green posterboard. Cut it out and draw funny looking eyes on it. This is the crazy grape! Have the Fruit Finder give the crazy grape to a child to hold while the Fruit Finder is taking a turn. This is the next Fruit Finder.

Make extra crazy grapes from the remaining green posterboard. Leave out the eyes! On the back of each grape print the syllables *Gr* and *ape*. At the end of the activity give one to each child to take home. The children can draw in their own crazy eyes.

COLOR WHACK

MATERIALS

White paper, crayons, tape, fly swatter.

PREPARATION

Color sheets of paper making two of each color. Primary colors are best in the beginning. Secure papers on a wall with the color-side face down.

LEARNING CIRCLE ACTIVITY

1. The children are looking for matching colors.
2. Have one child turn over two sheets of paper and place them on the floor.
3. If it is a match, the Learning Circle yells "whack!"
4. The Color Whacker whacks the two colors with a fly swatter.
5. Tape these back on the wall face-up. If a match is not made, another child takes a turn.
6. Repeat until all the papers on the wall are face-up.

MATERIALS FOR EXPANDING KNOWLEDGE

Paper, crayons, tape.

EXPANDING KNOWLEDGE

Play this activity as a memory game. Prepare smaller sized color cards so that many can be put on the wall. When a match is made, take them down and let the child keep them.

Use matching shapes, numbers, or letters to play this game.

MATERIALS FOR TEACHING TIPS

Red posterboard, felt marker, scissors.

TEACHING TIPS

Cut out round circles from the red posterboard. Print the word *Bong* on each circle. Place a *Bong* circle on the floor in front of each child. When a match is not made, have everyone slap their *Bong Buttons* and yell "bong!" Involving the entire class keeps everyone focused!

ICE CREAM MAKER

MATERIALS

Construction paper, felt pens, scissors, a box, white posterboard, tape.

PREPARATION

Print the words Ice Cream Store on the posterboard. Draw an ice cream cone at the bottom of the posterboard. Cut at least twenty circles from different colored construction paper. These are the ice cream balls. Cut squares of construction paper and print the numbers from one to twenty on them. Place these numbers in a box.

LEARNING CIRCLE ACTIVITY

1. Select an Ice Cream Maker.
2. The Ice Cream Maker chooses a number from the box.
3. If the number eight is chosen, the Ice Cream Maker can choose eight ice cream balls and tape them on the cone.
4. Count how many scoops were placed on the cone.
5. Take the scoops off the cone and put them back in the box.
6. Choose the next Ice Cream Maker.
7. Print the number of scoops each child chose on a sheet of construction paper.
8. Who built the tallest cone? Who built the shortest cone?

MATERIALS FOR EXPANDING KNOWLEDGE

Glue, sandpaper, colored gravel, wax paper, black velvet material, fake fur.

EXPANDING KNOWLEDGE

Go wild with flavors! Draw brown spots on a pink circle for a cherry chocolate ball. Draw red stripes on a white circle for a candy cane ball. Draw patches of different colors on a white circle for a rainbow ball. Discuss the names of the ice cream balls with the children. Play a memory game. See who can remember the names of the flavors. Choose two children to become ice cream makers. Build two cones at the same time. The different heights of the cones easily demonstrates higher and lower number concepts. Make ice cream balls from a variety of textures. Make caramel from sandpaper, candy crunch from colored gravel glued onto paper, pineapple sherbet from wax paper taped over a yellow construction paper circle, licorice from black velvet material, and monster ice cream from fake fur material.

MATERIALS FOR TEACHING TIPS

A bell.

TEACHING TIPS

When each child completes a cone, they ring a bell. This is the bell to the ice cream truck ready to deliver more ice cream to the store.

BALLOON POPPER

MATERIALS

Balloons, paper, felt pens, scissors, white posterboard, tape.

PREPARATION

Draw a variety of shapes such as circles, squares, triangles, and rectangles on pieces of paper. Cut out each one and stuff it inside a balloon. Blow up the balloons. Draw identical shapes on the posterboard two inches apart.

LEARNING CIRCLE ACTIVITY

1. Choose the Balloon Popper.
2. Have this child pop a balloon and identify the shape.
3. The Balloon Popper finds the identical shape on the posterboard and tapes the shape next to it.

MATERIALS FOR EXPANDING KNOWLEDGE

Crayons.

EXPANDING KNOWLEDGE

Color the shapes that are in the balloons. If the balloon has a red triangle inside, color a red triangle on the posterboard. Match shapes and colors.

Use unusual shapes to match. Use teardrop shapes, fish shapes, lollipop shapes, and ghost shapes at Halloween!

MATERIALS FOR TEACHING TIPS

Balloons, felt pens, scissors.

TEACHING TIPS

Promise a surprise at the end of the activity. Give each child a balloon with a shape inside it. Tell them to pop the balloon at home and identify the shape. See who can remember the shape at the Learning Circle on the next day.

POPCORN COUNTING

MATERIALS

Popcorn, paper plates.

PREPARATION

Make popcorn!

LEARNING CIRCLE ACTIVITY

1. Place a plate of popcorn in front of each child.
2. Say the number one.
3. Everyone in the Learning Circle eats one piece of popcorn.
4. Ask the child on your left to say the number that comes after one.
5. Eat that many pieces of popcorn!
6. Continue counting in this manner until everyone has counted as high as they can.
7. Help the Learning Circle to count to twenty.
8. Eat twenty pieces of popcorn!

MATERIALS FOR EXPANDING KNOWLEDGE

Large frying pan, popcorn, oil, large sheet, butter, caramel sauce.

EXPANDING KNOWLEDGE

Pop popcorn in an open frying pan placed on a large sheet. This is a good experience for all five senses. The children can feel the unpopped kernels and the popped kernels. Listen to the noise. Watch the popcorn fly! Taste the popcorn plain. Taste the popcorn with butter. Taste the popcorn with caramel sauce. Which way do you like it best? (*Warning*: close adult supervision is needed around the hot pan and hot oil.)

MATERIALS FOR TEACHING TIPS

Posterboard, felt pens, tape.

TEACHING TIPS

Use a visual aid as an attention-grabber. Draw a large open mouth on a posterboard. Tell the children that when they see a piece of popcorn in this mouth, they can eat the rest of their popcorn. When you have finished counting with the children, tape a piece of popcorn in the mouth. See who notices first. It won't take long!

TEXTURED ALPHABET

MATERIALS

Colored posterboard, felt pens, scissors, glue, various textured objects, one for each letter.

PREPARATION

Print alphabet letters on the posterboard. Cut out each letter. Suggestions for textures are cover the letter *B* with bandaids, the letter *C* with colored cotton balls, the letter *T* with tin foil, the letter *F* with fur, the letter *S* with satin, or the letter *P* with pipe cleaners.

LEARNING CIRCLE ACTIVITY

1. Introduce a letter of the alphabet.
2. With the children, cover that letter with a textured object that begins with that letter.
3. After each letter is introduced, display it on a wall. Add a new letter each week.

EXPANDING KNOWLEDGE

Ask the children for their ideas to cover each letter. Have the children in the Learning Circle close their eyes. See who can remember what object is covering a specific letter.

MATERIALS FOR TEACHING TIPS

White posterboard, felt pens.

TEACHING TIPS

When you are discussing ideas for covering a particular letter display a white posterboard. Drawn on this posterboard is a long inchworm 4 inches wide and the length of the board. Draw two large eyes and eyeglasses! Divide the body of the worm into the same number of segments as there are children. When a child thinks of an idea for a possible texture, he or she chooses a felt pen and marks an X in one of the segments. When all the segments are marked, they have sharpened their minds and have become smarter!

MYSTERY SOUNDS

MATERIALS

White posterboard, scissors, felt pens, identical opaque cans with lids, small objects. Suggested objects are dried beans, marbles, rubber bands, paper clips, gravel, buttons, and cotton balls.

PREPARATION

Place similar objects in each can. For example, place marbles in one can and gravel in another can. Cut the posterboard into small cards. Draw a picture on each card that matches the objects in the cans.

LEARNING CIRCLE ACTIVITY

1. Show the children the objects inside each can.
2. Put the lids on and mix them up.
3. Have the children shake the cans.
4. Who can tell what is in each can by listening to the sound it makes?
5. Who can place the pictures in front of the correct cans?
6. Remove the lids and see if a match was made.

MATERIALS FOR EXPANDING KNOWLEDGE

Cans from home.

EXPANDING KNOWLEDGE

Each child can bring a can from home with a hidden item inside. The Learning Circle guesses what is in each can.

This activity can be played by two children. One child mixes up the cans and the other child matches the pictures.

TEACHING TIPS

Twist your earlobes and turn your hearing on high! You will need full power for this activity.

DIP TREATS

MATERIALS

Paper plates, bowls, a variety of fruit, a selection of dips. Suggested dips are brown sugar, jam, coconut, chopped nuts, cinnamon, honey, chocolate sauce, sour cream, yogurt, or mustard!

PREPARATION

Place dips in separate bowls. Cut up fruit into small pieces.

LEARNING CIRCLE ACTIVITY

1. Distribute the paper plates and place the fruit and dips around the Learning Circle.
2. The children place a selection of fruit on their plates.
3. They experiment and observe how the taste of each fruit changes with different dips.

EXPANDING KNOWLEDGE

The children mix the remaining fruit together. How does it taste? Can you taste the different fruit? What taste do you like the best?

Taste the fruit and dips with eyes shut. Can you taste the fruit better? Does it taste any different?

MATERIALS FOR TEACHING TIPS

Marshmallows.

TEACHING TIPS

Save a special treat for last. Hide it in a bag. When the activity is over, pass out marshmallows! Let the children choose their favorite dip to put on their marshmallow.

TRAIN CONDUCTOR

MATERIALS

White posterboard, yellow paper, scissors, felt pens, magazines, a box, tape.

PREPARATION

Draw a train zig-zagging from left to right on the posterboard. Number each car from one to twenty. Cut out animal pictures from magazines and tape them onto the bottom of the posterboard. Cut out tickets from yellow paper. Number the tickets from one to twenty. Place the tickets in a box.

LEARNING CIRCLE ACTIVITY

1. Select a Train Conductor.
2. Have the Train Conductor choose a ticket from the box.
3. If the ticket reads ten, the Train Conductor picks an animal "passenger" and tapes it on car number ten.
4. Repeat until all the animals are on the train.

EXPANDING KNOWLEDGE

Introduce different passengers throughout the year. Use people, fruit, or ocean animals!

TEACHING TIPS

As each Train Conductor seats a passenger, he or she pulls an imaginary train whistle and the Learning Circle says "Choo Choo!"

FEELING FEET

MATERIALS

A large sheet, various textured objects. Suggested ideas are sandpaper, wood, netting, cardboard, carpet, sand, tissue paper, and waxpaper.

PREPARATION

Spread out the objects on a large sheet placed on the floor. Everyone takes off their shoes.

LEARNING CIRCLE ACTIVITY

1. Tell the children that they are going to feel with their feet instead of their hands.
2. Have everyone walk on the different textures in their bare feet.

EXPANDING KNOWLEDGE

Place one textured object on the sheet. See who can identify the object with their eyes closed!

At the Learning Circle, ask for a description of the experience.

How did the carpet feel?
Did you like walking on sandpaper?
What did you enjoy walking on the most?

TEACHING TIPS

Tell the children that wiggly feet are talking feet. The quietest feet will go first.

LADYBUG NUMBERS

MATERIALS

Red, yellow, and green posterboard, a black felt pen, scissors, tape.

PREPARATION

Cut out ten round circles about two inches in diameter from the red, yellow, and green posterboard. Draw a line down the middle of each circle and add black dots. Print a number from one to ten on the under-side of each circle. Cut out a large green leaf from the green posterboard. Tape the ladybugs on the leaf.

LEARNING CIRCLE ACTIVITY

1. Select a child to be the Ladybug Picker.
2. This child chooses a ladybug from the leaf and shows the number to the class.
3. The Ladybug Picker chooses a volunteer to identify the number.
4. If the volunteer correctly identifies the number, he or she picks out the next ladybug. If the number is not correctly identified, another volunteer is chosen.
5. Continue until everyone has had a turn choosing a ladybug.

EXPANDING KNOWLEDGE

Start with the numbers from one to ten. When the Learning Circle can recognize these numbers, add five more ladybugs with the numbers eleven to fifteen on them. As new numbers are learned, add more ladybugs!

Study the ladybugs when you introduce this activity. Explain that ladybugs can be red, yellow, or green!

Ask the children if anyone has a nickname. Talk about some of the nicknames in the Learning Circle. The name ladybug is a nickname. The ladybug's real name is Lady Bird Beetle!

TEACHING TIPS

Ask the children to sit quietly during the ladybug counting. If you scare them, they might crawl off the leaf and get lost in the classroom!

In the morning before the children arrive move the ladybugs to a different position on the leaf. Everyone can look for the ladybugs' new home each morning.

LADYBUG CARD GAME

MATERIALS

Red, yellow, and green posterboard, a black felt pen, scissors, clear contact paper.

PREPARATION

Make fifty-three ladybugs! Cut out fifty-three round circles about two inches in diameter from the colored posterboard. Draw a line down the middle of each circle and add black dots. Print the numbers from one to fifty on the under-side of each ladybug. Print the words *Lucky Bug*, on the remaining three. Cover the ladybugs with contact paper on both sides.

LEARNING CIRCLE ACTIVITY

1. This is a memory-matching game. Arrange the ladybugs in rows, number-side down, on the floor.
2. Have one child choose two ladybugs and turn them over.
3. If any of the digits match, the child keeps the pair. A 25 can match with a 45 because the number 5 appears on both ladybugs.
4. If a Lucky Bug is turned over, it can match with any number.
5. After the first child takes a turn whether a match is made or not, it is the next child's turn.
6. When all of the ladybugs have been matched, everyone counts their pairs!

EXPANDING KNOWLEDGE

Use the ladybugs at the Learning Circle to review numbers or to discuss calendar days. Show the number fifteen. Today is the fifteenth of November. What will tomorrow be? Show the ladybug numbered sixteen.

TEACHING TIPS

Praise each child when a match is found. Stress the idea that you play games to have fun and to enjoy the company of your friends.

COLOR CIRCLE

MATERIALS

White butcher paper, a felt pen, tape.

PREPARATION

Draw a large circle on the butcher paper and secure it to a wall. The children bring small objects in a specific color from home. For example, they bring blue objects from home for "blue week." Suggested color objects are scarves, ribbons, thread, scraps of material, napkins, hand towels, magazine pictures, coloring book pictures, or small toys.

LEARNING CIRCLE ACTIVITY

1. Ask the children, in turn, to bring their objects to the teacher.
2. Tape these objects inside the Color Circle. Many shades of the color will be evident!
3. Change the color theme every two weeks.

MATERIALS FOR EXPANDING KNOWLEDGE

Blue sticky stars.

EXPANDING KNOWLEDGE

Talk about the color blue. Ask questions that encourage answers. Where are the clouds? Where does a ship float? Act out blue ideas like, blue flowers, the ocean, blueberries, a blue crayon, blue buttons, or blue on someone's shirt.

Walk around the classroom and let everyone put a blue sticky star on something that is blue.

TEACHING TIPS

Keep blue interest alive! When a child brings in a blue object, let him or her share it at the Learning Circle. When it goes in the Color Circle, everyone can applaud!

FLY SWATTER

MATERIALS

White butcher paper, tape, felt pens, fly swatter.

PREPARATION

Secure a large sheet of butcher paper on a wall. Draw fifteen large flies on the paper. On the body of each fly draw a different shape. Suggestions are a circle, a rectangle, a triangle, an oval, a star, a diamond, a heart, a half moon, a cylinder, an octagon, a teardrop, a clover, a cresent moon, or a square.

LEARNING CIRCLE ACTIVITY

1. Choose a child to be the Fly Swatter.
2. Have the Fly Swatter stand in front of the fly paper.
3. Hand him or her a fly swatter.
4. Tell the Learning Circle that they are the flies who got away!
5. They buzz to warn the other flies.
6. Have them buzz until the Fly Swatter swats a fly on the paper.
7. The Fly Swatter then identifies the shape on the fly.

EXPANDING KNOWLEDGE

Draw letters or numbers on the flies. Play this activity when the class is learning about insects. Study the fly!

MATERIALS FOR TEACHING TIPS

Scissors.

TEACHING TIPS

Promise a fly at the end of the activity. Let each child cut out a fly from the paper and take it home.

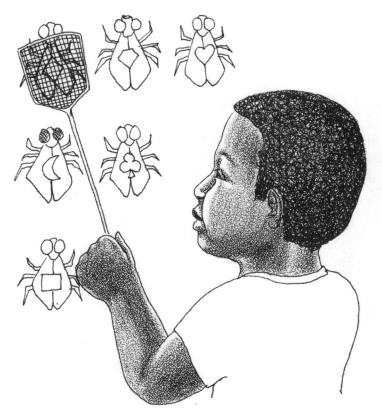

SPELL BOX

MATERIALS

A box, felt pens, scissors, posterboard, a knife, objects that are simple to spell. Suggested objects are a ball, a toy car, animals with short names, a nut, a piece of gum, and a can.

PREPARATION

Using felt pens print alphabet letters on the sides of the box. Place a selection of objects inside the box. Cut a hole larger than a fist on one side of the box. Make alphabet flashcards from posterboard with enough letters to spell the objects.

LEARNING CIRCLE ACTIVITY

1. Display the Spell Box.
2. Have a child reach into the box through the hole and pull out an object.
3. Help the children sound out the spelling of the object.
4. The child who chose the object uses the flashcards to spell the word.
5. Introduce the Spell Box often. Change the objects often!

MATERIALS FOR EXPANDING KNOWLEDGE

Photographs of each child, balloons.

EXPANDING KNOWLEDGE

Collect photographs of each child. Place the pictures inside the Spell Box. Have someone pull out a picture and identify the child. This child spells his or her name with the flashcards.

Place a variety of balloons inside the box. Help the children spell the color of the balloon.

MATERIALS FOR TEACHING TIPS

A box, felt pens, scissors, stickers, pennies, balloons.

TEACHING TIPS

Promise a surprise at the end of the activity. Display a box labeled Special Spell Box. Pull a special object from the box. Help the children sound out the letters. Spell the word with the flashcards. Make it a special treat! Suggested treats are stickers, pennies, balloons, or a special snack.

WEATHER ART

MATERIALS

Colored posterboard, white paper, tape, felt pens, scissors.

PREPARATION

In the middle of the posterboard secure a sheet of white paper. Cut out wordstrips from another sheet of paper. Write weather conditions on the wordstrips. Pictures are helpful, too. Examples of weather words are:

Sunny	Foggy
Windy	Snowy
Rainy	Thunder
Cloudy	Rainbow
Stormy	Frosty

LEARNING CIRCLE ACTIVITY

1. Choose one child from the Learning Circle.
2. This child observes the weather and chooses the appropriate wordstrip.
3. Stress the first letter sound of the weather word.
4. If the word *Sunny* was chosen, place this wordstrip at the top of the paper.
5. Then the child draws a picture of the weather on the paper.

EXPANDING KNOWLEDGE

Instead of placing only the wordstrip above the paper print the words, A_____ day, above the paper. Place the wordstrip on the blank. The children will become familiar with these words and will be able to read them with you.

If the weather changes during the day, the weather person can change the weather and picture.

TEACHING TIPS

While the weather person is drawing the weather picture, the other children can finger draw! If a rainbow is the picture, draw the shape of a rainbow in the air or on the floor with your finger. Draw a rainbow on your hand! Draw a rainbow on the back of the person sitting next to you.

ROPE PERSON

MATERIALS

A rope, colored yarn, scissors.

PREPARATION

Cut a string of colored yarn about three feet long.

LEARNING CIRCLE ACTIVITY

1. Select a child to be the Rope Person.
2. Give the Rope Person a long rope.
3. Have the Rope Person manipulate the shape of the rope to form a letter on the floor.
4. The Rope Person can use the shorter piece of yarn to help form a letter.

EXPANDING KNOWLEDGE

Each child can make the first letter in their name. Make rope numbers and shapes!

TEACHING TIPS

During this activity hang up strings of yarn in different colors. At the end of the activity everyone can choose a piece of colored yarn and take it home. The children can play rope writing at home.

TWIN FINDER

MATERIALS

White posterboard, paper, felt pens, scissors, tape, a box.

PREPARATION

Draw a large spaceship on the posterboard. On the spaceship draw fifteen Martians and a round red circle. Label the circle *Blast Off!* Draw the Martians as stick figures with different shapes for heads. Suggested shapes are a circle, a square, a rectangle, a triangle, an oval, a star, a diamond, a heart, a half moon, a cresent moon, an octagon, a cylinder, a teardrop, a clover, or a pear. Color each of the shapes a different color.

Draw fifteen Martians on white posterboard and cut them out. Draw the same shapes and colors for their heads as the Martians on the spaceship. Place these Martians in a box. Call this box the *Lost Ship Box.*

LEARNING CIRCLE ACTIVITY

1. Choose a child to be the Twin Finder.
2. The Twin Finder chooses a Martian from the box and searches the spaceship for the twin.
3. Tape the Martian next to its twin matching shape and color.

EXPANDING KNOWLEDGE

Vary the shades of color of the Martians. If a light green Martian is on the spaceship, draw a dark green Martian for the Lost Space Box and match shades of the same color.

Discuss the different shapes. Think of objects that have similar shapes. Take a walk around the classroom and look for identical shapes.

Play this activity when the class is learning about space. Pretend to be up in space. Look out the windows of the spaceship. What is in outer space?

Let the children play with the Twin Finder activity by themselves. It offers a good source for independent play.

TEACHING TIPS

Tell the children that at the end of the activity, everyone will take a ride on the spaceship. When everyone is ready, push the button labeled *Blast Off.*

EYEBALL SOUP

MATERIALS

White posterboard, green posterboard, construction paper, felt pens, tape, scissors.

PREPARATION

Draw a large circle on the white posterboard. This is a soup bowl. Print the word *Menu* at the top of the posterboard.

Draw eight frogs on the green posterboard each with a different set of eyes. Draw the eyes looking up, looking down, to the left, to the right, opened, shut, cross-eyed, and winking. Cut them out and tape them near the soup bowl.

Print eight words on strips of construction paper that describe the sets of eyes. Tape these near the frogs. These words are up, down, left, right, open, shut, goofy, and wink.

LEARNING CIRCLE ACTIVITY

1. Choose a Witch or Wizard!
2. This child chooses a frog and tapes it on the soup bowl.
3. Then the Witch or Wizard finds the word-strip that describes the eyes that are on the cooking frog.
4. Stress the first letter sound of the matching word to assist the Witch or Wizard.
5. Tape this word under the word *Menu* on the posterboard.

EXPANDING KNOWLEDGE

Color code this activity! Use the same color construction paper for the winking frog and the word wink.

Use rabbits at Easter and place them in an Easter basket. Use fish when you are learning about the ocean and place them in a fish bowl!

MATERIALS FOR TEACHING TIPS

Posterboard, felt pens.

TEACHING TIPS

During this activity give each child a card made from posterboard. Print the word *Menu* on each card. Have the children draw the eyeballs.

WORM FINDER

MATERIALS

Brown construction paper, white poster-board, felt pens, scissors, crayons, a box.

PREPARATION

Cut or tear the brown paper into shreds. This is the dirt that the worms live in. Cut out twenty worms from the posterboard. Color five worms red, five worms yellow, five worms blue, and five worms green. Place the shredded paper and the worms in a box. Mix them up!

LEARNING CIRCLE ACTIVITY

1. Choose the Worm Finder!
2. Have this child search through the box and pull out a worm.
3. Then the Worm Finder searches for a second worm of identical color.
4. If a worm is found that is not a match, place it back in the box.
5. Continue until two identical worms have been found.

MATERIALS FOR EXPANDING KNOWLEDGE

White posterboard, felt pens.

EXPANDING KNOWLEDGE

Color the worms in shades of different colors. All the blue shades will make a match.

Display a sign that says *Worm Hunt: One Red Worm and Two Yellow Worms.* Search for the worms that are described on the sign.

Draw a fishing pole on a posterboard. Print a number on each worm. Have each child find a worm. The child who is holding the number one worm will tape the worm on the fishing hook. The child with the number two worm will tape that worm above the number one worm. Continue up the line until everyone has had a turn taping their worm on the fishing pole. Count the number of worms!

Print the letter *W* on five of the worms. Print the letter *O* and *R* and *M* on the other fifteen worms. Have the Worm Finder search for four worms that spell the word *Worm.*

TEACHING TIPS

Have everyone say this verse at the start of this activity. Move your fingers like wiggly worms!

Worm, worm, wiggle, wiggle,
Hiding in the ground.
Worm, worm, wiggle, wiggle,
Move your hand around!

Repeat this verse as each new Worm Finder begins the search.

MYSTERY MIX

MATERIALS

Paper plates, spoons, forks, various food items such as apples, bananas, nuts, raisins, muffins, yogurt, or crackers.

PREPARATION

Collect the various food items and bring them to the Learning Circle.

LEARNING CIRCLE ACTIVITY

1. Create an original food dish.
2. Have each child choose a food item that they would like to put in the Mystery Mix.
3. Place a small sample of this food item on everyone's plate.
4. Have each child think of a name for their own Mystery Mix.
5. Taste!

EXPANDING KNOWLEDGE

What food could you put on cottage cheese or lettuce? What sounds good on a cracker or a slice of bread? Try the ideas at snack time!

MATERIALS FOR TEACHING TIPS

A small bell.

TEACHING TIPS

You are the Waiter who is taking the orders for the Mystery Mix. As each child names a food item, he or she rings a small bell. Everyone yells "Waiter!"

MAGICIAN

MATERIALS

A table, a sheet, a paper bag, a wooden spoon, foil, various objects. Suggested objects are a small stuffed animal, a candle, a plastic flower, a comb, and a mitten.

PREPARATION

Place five objects on the table. Make a magic wand by wrapping a wooden spoon in foil.

LEARNING CIRCLE ACTIVITY

1. Choose the Magician.
2. Have the Magician stand behind the table.
3. Have the rest of the children look at and touch the objects.
4. Then the children sit down in the Learning Circle.
5. Cover the objects with a sheet.

6. Hold up the sheet slightly at two corners so only the Magician can see the objects.
7. Have the Magician choose an object and slip it into a paper bag.
8. When the Magician waves the magic wand, the children say the magic words,

   Abracadabra, bones and hair.
   Find the object that's not there!

9. Pull the sheet away.
10. Ask who can tell what object is missing.
11. After each incorrect guess the Magician can offer a clue.
12. The child who gives the correct answer becomes the Magician.

EXPANDING KNOWLEDGE

Increase the number of objects on the table as their memory skills increase.

Try this activity with one child at a time. The child studies two objects. Blindfold the child and take one object away. The child feels the remaining object and guesses what object is still on the table. What object is missing?

TEACHING TIPS

While the children are studying the objects, help them to focus their thinking. Ask questions like:

Do you see the seashell?
Is it between the teddybear and the tangerine?
Do you have a piggy bank?
The Easter Bunny must have forgotten that plastic egg!

Talking about the objects will help the children to remember them.

WISH PERSON

MATERIALS

Crystal marbles, a box, sticky stars.

PREPARATION

Decorate a Wish Box with sticky stars. Place a selection of crystal marbles inside the box.

LEARNING CIRCLE ACTIVITY

1. Choose a child to be the Wish Person.
2. Have this child choose a marble and show it to the class.

3. The Wish Person holds the marble and makes three wishes.
4. These wishes are made aloud so that the entire class can share the experience. The Wish Person is learning to verbalize his or her thoughts and the children are learning to listen!

EXPANDING KNOWLEDGE

Make a wish for someone else or make Christmas wishes! Make imagination wishes like, if you could turn yourself into an animal, what would it be?

MATERIALS FOR TEACHING TIPS

A large marble.

TEACHING TIPS

The Wish Person places a large marble in front of a child who was listening quietly. This child becomes the next Wish Person.

THE NAME GAME

MATERIALS

Colored construction paper, felt pens, scissors, tape, a box.

PREPARATION

Print each child's name on a sheet of construction paper. Cover each letter separately with a small piece of paper taped onto the construction paper. In small print write the name of each child on the construction paper. This will tell the teacher whose name is on each paper. Display these on a wall.

Print the letters from everyone's name on squares of paper. Place these letters in a box.

LEARNING CIRCLE ACTIVITY

1. Each child, in turn, takes one letter from the letter box.
2. If the letter *A* is drawn, the teacher flips up and secures all the pieces of paper that have the letter *A* under them.
3. When enough letters have been turned over, their names will begin to appear.
4. The children will begin to guess where their names are.

EXPANDING KNOWLEDGE

Try a name scramble! Print a child's name on a sheet of construction paper. Print the first letter of their name larger than the rest of the letters and in a different color. Cut each letter out. Tape the letters of a child's name on a sheet of paper but scramble them up! The children search for their names and place the letters in the right order. Guide each child by reminding them to look for the first letter in their name. Give clues concerning its position on the wall. Tell them the color of their first letter. Help them to discover it themselves! That way it builds confidence and fosters a sense of achievement.

MATERIALS FOR TEACHING TIPS

A kazoo, a party horn, or a tambourine.

TEACHING TIPS

Before a letter is flipped over, make a fun or exciting noise. Blow on a kazoo or a party horn! Shake a tambourine for an attention-grabber.

SECRET WORD GAME

MATERIALS

None

PREPARATION

None

LEARNING CIRCLE ACTIVITY

1. Whisper a secret word to each child in the Learning Circle.
2. Ask them to try to remember their secret word.
3. Call a second Learning Circle later in the morning.
4. Who can remember their secret word? (This is a good way to end a Learning Circle.)

EXPANDING KNOWLEDGE

The secret words can relate to a topic of study. If the children are learning about space, use star, moon, sun, Mars, and spaceship. If the topic is colors, use color words. Let the children choose a theme!

MATERIALS FOR TEACHING TIPS

Posterboard, felt pens, sticky stars.

TEACHING TIPS

During the second Learning Circle display a posterboard that has the names of the children and the secret words printed on it. Help the children to remember their words by offering clues. The children place a sticky star by their names when they remember.

BOUNCING BALLS

MATERIALS

None

PREPARATION

Learn the story.

LEARNING CIRCLE ACTIVITY

1. This is a visual imagery game. You are going to tell the children a story while they shut their eyes.
2. Ask the children to close their eyes.
3. Tell them to make pictures in their minds while you slowly tell a story. This is the story:

> You are on the street where you live. You see your house and your neighbors' homes. You also see a giant yellow ball as big as a van bouncing down the street. It is as bright as the sun! Behind that is a green ball bouncing down the street. It is bouncing higher than the houses! Here comes a blue ball. It is rolling down the street. It is rolling very fast. There is one more ball coming. It is a red ball. It is bouncing towards your house. It has stopped by the front door. It is bouncing against the door! Open the door and you see two letters on the ball. The letters are *h* and *i*. These two letters spell the word *hi*.

4. The children open their eyes.
5. Ask questions about the story.
   Who can remember the color of the ball that was as big as a van?
   What was the color of the ball that could bounce higher than your house?
   What ball rolled down the street?
   What letters were on it?
   What did the letters spell?

MATERIALS FOR EXPANDING KNOWLEDGE

Paper, crayons.

EXPANDING KNOWLEDGE

Place a piece of paper and a yellow, green, blue, and red crayon in front of each child. They draw a ball. Ask them to find a yellow crayon and color it. They draw another ball. Ask them to find a green crayon and color it. Continue in this manner until the four balls in the story have been colored. Tell them they can draw more balls and choose different colors to color them. This activity will tell you who knows their colors and who needs help.

TEACHING TIPS

This activity is best conducted in a quiet atmosphere. Dim the lights. Offer the option of laying down. Speak slowly but with enthusiasm. Set guidelines. If you talk or wiggle, you will not be able to see the bouncing balls!

Visual imagery games increase one's ability to form strong mental pictures. They increase memory skills and help to develop creative, inventive thinking. They are relaxing and restful, prime conditions for learning.

TREASURE CHEST

MATERIALS

None

PREPARATION

Learn the story.

LEARNING CIRCLE ACTIVITY

1. This is a visual imagery game.
2. Tell the children to close their eyes and make pictures in their minds while you slowly tell a story.
3. The children can act out the story with arm movements. This is the story:

   You are on a rowboat, out in the middle of the ocean. You are rowing slowly. Put the oars down and put on your underwater mask. Dive into the ocean. The water feels so cold! Kick your legs faster. Swim towards the bottom of the ocean. The water feels warmer now. You see many beautiful things—fish, seashells, and a pink starfish. Then you see a treasure chest! It is bright red. Swim over to the treasure chest. Try to push the lid up. Push harder! It opened! Take a look inside.

4. Now the children open their eyes. What did you see in the treasure chest? Let each child have a turn to say what they saw.

MATERIALS FOR EXPANDING KNOWLEDGE

Paper, paint, paintbrushes.

EXPANDING KNOWLEDGE

Play this activity when the children are studying the ocean. Look for sea-life that you have discussed.

The children can paint an underwater picture of things they saw during the Treasure Chest activity. Talk about each picture in another Learning Circle.

TEACHING TIPS

During this activity tell the children that if they listen carefully, they will find something exciting! If someone disturbs our ocean trip, they will have to sit on dry land. Point to a nearby chair!

PUPPY COUNTING

MATERIALS

None

PREPARATION

Learn the Story.

LEARNING CIRCLE ACTIVITY

1. This is a visual imagery game.
2. The children close their eyes and make pictures in their minds while you slowly tell a story. This is the story:

> You see a large box sitting on the floor. It is starting to shake! You can see a floppy ear at the top of the box. It is a puppy! It is jumping out of the box! Now it is resting on the floor. It has fallen asleep. Here comes another puppy. You can see its nose at the top of the box. It is jumping out of the box! Now there are two puppies asleep on the floor. Another puppy is sliding down the box. Now there are three puppies! Look at the box again. There is a tail coming over the top. The puppy is coming out backwards! Now there are four puppies on the floor. Is that all the puppies? No! The box is shaking! You can see a paw at the top of the box. The puppy is jumping out. Now there are five puppies asleep on the floor.

3. The children open their eyes. Ask the questions:

> How many puppies jumped out of the box?
> What parts of the puppies did you see at the top of the box?
> What did the puppies do when they reached the floor?

EXPANDING KNOWLEDGE

Imagine an animal box. Different animals jump out of the box. See who can remember the kinds of animals! The puppies or the different animals can jump back into the box. Count backwards from five to one.

TEACHING TIPS

The puppies will not come out if we are too noisy! Let's lay quietly and count how many puppies will come out.

ROBOT READER

MATERIALS

White posterboard, felt pens, construction paper, scissors, tape, a ruler, a styrofoam ball, foil.

PREPARATION

Draw and color a large robot on the poster-board. Display it on a wall. Add many colorful buttons. Label one of the buttons *Start*. Make a microphone. Secure a styro-foam ball at the top of a ruler. Wrap the ball and ruler in foil. As an option buy a toy microphone available at most toy stores. Print a word such as *Dog* on a strip of construction paper and tape it on the robot. Begin with simple three letter words. Change the degree of difficulty as necessary.

LEARNING CIRCLE ACTIVITY

1. Choose the Robot Reader.
2. The Robot Reader pushes the *Start* button and says into the microphone, "I am a robot and I can read the word *Dog*."
3. Change the robot word once a week.

EXPANDING KNOWLEDGE

Have the robot words relate to a topic that you are studying. Print the words moon, star, planet, and Mars for space; red, green, blue, and yellow for colors; ant, bee, fly, and ladybug for insects; and fish, whale, sea, and water for the ocean.

Try using the children's names. Ask the children for word ideas!

TEACHING TIPS

Label a button on the robot *Quiet*. The Robot Reader pushes the *Quiet* button when the Learning Circle needs a quiet reminder. Explain that the robot will not work prop-erly if it is disturbed by loud air waves!

NAME MAKER

MATERIALS

White posterboard, felt pens, scissors, tape.

PREPARATION

Draw the face of a baby on the posterboard. Cut it out. Make letter flashcards from the remaining posterboard. On one flashcard put a two letter word ending such as *am, og,* or *un.* Put consonants that will complete a word on the other flashcards.

LEARNING CIRCLE ACTIVITY

1. Display the face of the baby.
2. Tape a flashcard with a word ending under the face.
3. Display the letter flashcards.
4. Select a Name Maker.
5. Have the Name Maker choose a letter and tape it in front of the two letter flashcard. If the flashcard *og* is under the face and the letter *F* was chosen, the baby's name is going to be *Fog!* Change the baby's name every morning. Change the two letter flashcard every week.

EXPANDING KNOWLEDGE

Change this activity so that it relates to certain holidays. Name a ghost for Halloween, a turkey for Thanksgiving, a reindeer for Christmas, and a bunny for Easter.

Have everyone spell their name when they are Name Maker.

MATERIALS FOR TEACHING TIPS

Paper, felt pens, a box.

TEACHING TIPS

Print the alphabet letters on small pieces of paper. Place them inside a box. Have each child choose a letter. The child who chose the letter closest to the letter *A* can be Name Maker.

RIDDLE BOX

MATERIALS

Various pictures, magazines, scissors, a box, felt pens.

PREPARATION

Decorate a Riddle Box with question marks on the sides. Cut out magazine pictures and place them in a box. Suggested pictures are animals, food, insects, household objects, and outdoor objects such as, the sun, a tree, or a swimming pool.

LEARNING CIRCLE ACTIVITY

1. One child chooses a picture from the Riddle Box.
2. Have this child look at the picture without showing it to the rest of the class.
3. Help this child give clues about the picture.
4. After each clue see if anyone can guess what the picture is.

EXPANDING KNOWLEDGE

Use only one word to describe the picture! If the picture is a pig, say only the word pink, then snout, then mud, and then farm.

The pictures can have a common theme. If the children are learning about the ocean, use fish and sea-life pictures.

MATERIALS FOR TEACHING TIPS

Colored envelopes.

TEACHING TIPS

During this activity display a special riddle hidden in a colored envelope. At the end of this activity choose a good listener to look at the picture and give clues to the rest of the class.

STORYTELLER

MATERIALS

A pencil or ruler, a small styrofoam ball, tape, foil.

PREPARATION

Make a microphone by placing a styrofoam ball on the end of a pencil or ruler. Wrap it in foil.

LEARNING CIRCLE ACTIVITY

1. Select a Storyteller.
2. The Storyteller talks to the class for three minutes using the microphone.
3. Suggest topics such as families, vacations, favorite things to do, or pets.
4. The Storyteller can ask the other children questions:

    What is your favorite color?
    What do you like to eat?
    What is your favorite TV show?

    This activity encourages a child to lead!

EXPANDING KNOWLEDGE

The class can ask the Storyteller questions. Give the Storyteller the option of singing a song or leading the class in a song. The Storyteller can make a noise and ask who can identify the noise. For a child who enjoys making wishes suggest a full three minutes of wishing!

TEACHING TIPS

Ask the children if they sit very still when they are watching their favorite TV show. Tell them to sit that still when the Storyteller is speaking.

MYSELF

MATERIALS

Butcher paper, white paper, felt pens, crayons, tape.

PREPARATION

Secure a large sheet of butcher paper on a wall. Draw a large circle on the butcher paper. This is the earth. Draw land forms on the circle. Have the children color the earth.

LEARNING CIRCLE ACTIVITY

1. Distribute crayons and paper to each child.
2. Have the children draw a picture of themselves on a sheet of white paper.
3. When they have finished, have them tape their pictures around the outside of the earth.

MATERIALS FOR EXPANDING KNOWLEDGE

A mirror, a tape recorder, paint, paper.

EXPANDING KNOWLEDGE

Discuss the idea that there is no one on the earth who is exactly like each one of them. What makes everyone different? Pass a mirror around the Learning Circle. Everyone looks different! Have everyone say their name into a tape recorder. Everyone sounds different. Make a paint blot on a piece of paper. Ask each child to tell you about the design. Everyone thinks and sees things differently.

TEACHING TIPS

After each child places his or her picture on the earth, they say, "Nobody is just like me. I'm as special as can be." Applaud each child!

BUMPER STICKER

MATERIALS

White posterboard, felt pens, white construction paper, scissors, tape, a chair, a small horn such as a bicycle horn.

PREPARATION

Draw and color the back of a car with rear window, wheels, and bumper on the posterboard. Cut wordstrips from the construction paper. Print a word such as *Smile* on a wordstrip. This is the Bumper Sticker! Tape the Bumper Sticker on the car. Place a chair in front of the poster. This is the "class car."

LEARNING CIRCLE ACTIVITY

1. Choose a child to read the Bumper Sticker.
2. Have this child sit in the chair facing the poster.
3. The teacher reads the word to the class and discusses the letter sounds in the word.
4. Give this child a small horn.
5. This child reads the Bumper Sticker on the car and then honks the horn!

EXPANDING KNOWLEDGE

Print a popular saying on the bumper sticker. The children can watch for this bumper sticker as they ride in their own cars. Print a child's name on the bumper sticker. Print a word that relates to a topic you are studying.

TEACHING TIPS

After the Bumper Sticker reader has honked the horn, have the Learning Circle wave hello and say, "Hi!"

FLOWER POWER

MATERIALS

White paper, felt pens, crayons, tape.

PREPARATION

None

LEARNING CIRCLE ACTIVITY

1. Distribute paper, crayons, and felt pens to each child.
2. Each child draws a flower using a variety of felt pens.
3. Have them color the flowers with crayons.
4. Display the flowers on a wall.
5. Have each child find their flower and describe it.
6. Ask each child to give their flower a name.
7. Discuss the idea that each flower on the wall is different. No two flowers are alike. No two children are alike!

MATERIALS FOR EXPANDING KNOWLEDGE

Flowers.

EXPANDING KNOWLEDGE

Give each child a flower to hold. Notice how each flower is different. If each child has a different kind of flower, talk about the difference in the petals, the colors, the height, the scent, and the stem. If the flowers are the same kind, talk about the differences that are noticeable: the height, the color, the markings, and the petals.

MATERIALS FOR TEACHING TIPS

Flower stickers.

TEACHING TIPS

After everyone has talked about their flower, they can choose a flower sticker to stick on their picture.

HEART FELTS

MATERIALS

Felt material in a variety of colors, white posterboard, scissors, tape.

PREPARATION

Cut the felt into heart shapes. Tape the hearts on a posterboard. Display the poster-board at the Learning Circle. Cut one large red felt heart.

LEARNING CIRCLE ACTIVITY

1. Choose a child to hold the red felt heart.
2. Ask this child, "Why are you special?"
3. After this child has answered, he or she passes the heart to another child.
4. Ask this child, "Why are you special?"
5. Continue until everyone has answered the question.

MATERIALS FOR EXPANDING KNOWLEDGE

Posterboard, felt pens, a mirror, tape.

EXPANDING KNOWLEDGE

Draw the figure of a child on a posterboard. Tape a mirror where the face should be. Display the poster in the classroom. During the day ask different children to stand in front of the mirror and tell you why they feel special today, how they are feeling, or what they like about themselves. Display the poster periodically during the year.

TEACHING TIPS

Show the children the different colored felt hearts on the posterboard. After everyone has answered the question in the activity, have everyone choose a heart to take home. Encourage them to pass their heart to family members and ask, "Why are you special?"

COLOR CLUE

MATERIALS

White paper, felt pens, colored construction paper, tape, scissors.

PREPARATION

Draw simple pictures such as a flower, a fish, a rabbit, a snowman, a snake, or a kite on white paper. Make these pictures four inches by four inches. Cut a sheet of construction paper in half. Fold the remaining half over once. Now open it up. Tape the picture inside. Fold the top down so the picture cannot be seen. Repeat with all the pictures. Secure these on a wall.

LEARNING CIRCLE ACTIVITY

1. Have a child choose a hidden picture.
2. Show the picture only to this child.
3. Have the child act out the picture following the rules of charades.
4. When the picture has been guessed, ask what color the picture should be.

EXPANDING KNOWLEDGE

Next to each picture on the construction paper tape a white circle. Color it. After the picture has been guessed, its color has to be guessed! Have the children name different colors and when the color has been guessed, ask for the entire answer. A pink snowman! Add two colors. A pink and purple snowman! Make the answers funny. A blue and yellow dinosaur. A green and orange ghost. Use this activity to introduce new colors.

MATERIALS FOR TEACHING TIPS

Balloons.

TEACHING TIPS

Tell the children that they can take the picture home. Encourage them to play this game with their families using the picture.

Add a surprise to the game! Hide a balloon in your fist. The child who guesses the color can keep the balloon. Play until everyone has won.

I SPY

MATERIALS

Stickers, glitter, paint, paper tubes.

PREPARATION

Decorate one of the paper tubes with paint, glitter, and stickers. Foil tubes cut in half or rolled construction paper also make good tubes.

LEARNING CIRCLE ACTIVITY

1. Pass out small tubes to each child.
2. Choose the Spy Person.
3. Give the Spy Person the special decorated tube.
4. Have the Spy Person look through the viewer and find an object in the room.
5. Clues are offered to describe the object until someone guesses what has been spied.
6. The other children use their viewers to hunt for the object. When a child wants to make a guess, he or she yells, "I Spy _____!"

MATERIALS FOR EXPANDING KNOWLEDGE

Felt pens, paper, scissors, tape.

EXPANDING KNOWLEDGE

Play I Spy outside or during the different seasons. Display the names of the children around the classroom. The children can use their viewers to hunt for their name. When the children are learning about colors, spy colored objects in the classroom.

TEACHING TIPS

Spies make very quiet and silent movements. A noisy spy will not hear the clues!

STICKER PERSON

MATERIALS

White posterboard, paper, scissors, felt pens, stickers.

PREPARATION

Draw a picture such as a ladybug, a giraffe, or a dinosaur on a posterboard. Draw circles, the size of stickers, on the picture. Draw as many circles as there are days in the current month. These are the spots where the stickers will be placed.

Prepare a word wall by displaying wordstrips with words relating to the picture on the posterboard. If the picture is a ladybug, use the words red, black, spots, bug, Spring, grass, and fly!

LEARNING CIRCLE ACTIVITY

1. Display the sticker poster.
2. Each day select a Sticker Person who chooses from a variety of ·stickers.
3. Ask the Sticker Person to identify a word from the word wall. After a word has been identified, the Sticker Person places the sticker in a circle on the poster.

MATERIALS FOR EXPANDING KNOWLEDGE

Posterboard, felt pens.

EXPANDING KNOWLEDGE

Draw a different sticker poster each month! The poster becomes a familiar "friend." The children will enjoy saying goodbye to each poster, when a new one visits the classroom.

Hang wordstrips with the name of each child around the room. Have the Sticker Person search for his or her name before a sticker can be placed on the posterboard. Hang last names! Change their positions often.

TEACHING TIPS

Ask everyone to twist their earlobes and turn on their ears. Listen to the word that the Sticker Person is going to say.

HALLOWEEN SPIDER WEBS

MATERIALS

Black construction paper, white paper, a box, marbles, white yarn, white paint, felt pens, crayons, scissors, tape.

PREPARATION

Cut the construction paper to just cover the inside bottom of the box. Cut strings of yarn.

LEARNING CIRCLE ACTIVITY

1. Place a sheet of black construction paper in the box.
2. Place three teaspoons of white paint on the black paper.
3. Place two marbles in the box and tilt the box back and forth.
4. Watch a web form as the marbles spread the paint into thin lines.
5. Repeat with each child.
6. After the webs are made, have each child draw a spider on a sheet of white paper.
7. Color the spider and cut it out.
8. Tape one end of a piece of yarn to the web and the other end on the spider.

MATERIALS FOR EXPANDING KNOWLEDGE

A skein of yarn.

EXPANDING KNOWLEDGE

Discuss spiders and how they build their webs. Build a giant spider web! Tie one end of a skein of yarn to a heavy object in the classroom. Each child, in turn, takes the yarn and walks around the classroom wrapping the yarn around a stable object. When everyone has had a turn, look at the web.

Pretend to be spiders. Walk carefully through the maze. Draw and cut out a giant spider from construction paper. Throw the spider into the giant web. Pretend to be flies. Walk through the maze but stay away from the spider!

TEACHING TIPS

While the children are waiting for a turn to build the web, have them sing The Spider Web Song to the tune of "Mary Had A Little Lamb."

Spin a web and catch a bug,
Catch a bug, catch a bug.
Spin a web and catch a bug,
Spin a shiny web.

Catch a bug and eat it up,
Eat it up, eat it up,
Catch a bug and eat it up,
And then go straight to bed!

Use hand movements when singing this song. Point a finger and spin the other hand around it when singing "spin a web." Open your fist and close it in a catching motion when you sing "catch a bug." Bring your fingers to your mouth when you sing "eat it up." Rest your head on your hands for "straight to bed."

THANKSGIVING FEATHER TURKEYS

MATERIALS

Russet potatoes, feathers, red construction paper, colored toothpicks, scissors.

PREPARATION

Draw turkey heads with necks on the construction paper. Draw two tabs at the bottom of the necks. Cut them out.

LEARNING CIRCLE ACTIVITY

1. Give each child a potato, a turkey head, different colored feathers, and five toothpicks.
2. Position the turkey head on the potato.
3. Break one of the toothpicks in half.
4. Press each half through the neck tabs and down into the potato.
5. Use one of the remaining toothpicks to poke holes in the potato for the feathers.
6. Place the feathers into the holes.
7. Use the remaining four toothpicks for the legs of the turkey.

MATERIALS FOR EXPANDING KNOWLEDGE

Blocks, rocks, sticks.

EXPANDING KNOWLEDGE

Make a turkey farm! Group the turkeys together and place a fence around them using blocks, rocks, or sticks. Call this the turkey farm. Give the turkey farm a name.

Discuss turkeys and how they are raised. Would you want to be a turkey?

Have the children bring their turkeys home to use as a centerpiece at their Thanksgiving table.

MATERIALS FOR TEACHING TIPS

Posterboard, a felt pen, paper, tape.

TEACHING TIPS

During the turkey making display a posterboard. Print the word *Gobble* in large letters on the posterboard. Leave space between each letter. Print as many *Gobbles* as there are children. Cover each word with a piece of paper. When each child finishes their turkey, they can uncover a word to reveal *Gobble*. Each time this is done, announce that it is "Gobble time" and have everyone gobble like a turkey!

CHRISTMAS PRESENTS

MATERIALS

White construction paper, felt pens, crayons, ribbons, bows, sticky stars, glitter, glue, scissors.

PREPARATION

Cut up strips of ribbon measuring the length and width of the paper.

LEARNING CIRCLE ACTIVITY

1. Give each child a sheet of paper and tell them that they are going to design wrapping paper.
2. Have them draw and color designs on their paper. Possible wrapping paper designs are hearts, stripes, circles, flowers, rainbows, or ice cream cones!
3. The sticky stars, glitter, bows, and ribbons are the final touch to the designs.

EXPANDING KNOWLEDGE

Have the children share their "presents" at the Learning Circle. Every child can tell what is in their "present."

What could you use to wrap a present if you did not have any wrapping paper?

MATERIALS FOR TEACHING TIPS

Tiny, wrapped presents of balloons, nickels, and Christmas stickers.

TEACHING TIPS

During this activity display tiny wrapped presents. Let each child open a present after they finish their wrapping paper.

CHRISTMAS CALENDAR

MATERIALS

White construction paper, felt pens, crayons, cotton, glitter, glue, Christmas stickers, and a stapler.

PREPARATION

Draw a large Santa face on a nine inch by twelve inch sheet of construction paper. Draw one for each child. Draw a December calendar on another nine inch by twelve inch sheet of construction paper. Place a Christmas sticker on December twenty-fifth. Make one for each child.

LEARNING CIRCLE ACTIVITY

1. Have the children color their Santa Claus.
2. They can glue on cotton for his beard, moustache, and eyebrows and use the glitter where they want!
3. Staple their December calendar onto their Santa. Tell them to hang their calendars at home and every morning draw a large X over the correct date. They will be able to see the days move closer to Christmas and they will be printing the letter X!

MATERIALS FOR EXPANDING KNOWLEDGE

Construction paper, felt pens.

EXPANDING KNOWLEDGE

Make a December calendar for the classroom. Draw a Christmas ball in each square. Every morning one child colors the Christmas ball for that date. Draw Christmas trees or stars. Encourage them to count the days until Christmas!

MATERIALS FOR TEACHING TIPS

Christmas bells.

TEACHING TIPS

When the children complete their calendars, they can shake a row of Christmas bells.

EASTER BUNNY NESTS

MATERIALS

Paper plates, colored tissue paper, colored construction paper, scissors, felt pens, crayons, glue, large colored cotton balls.

PREPARATION

Draw eggs on many colors of construction paper. Draw at least two per child. Cut them out as squares of paper with an egg on each one. Draw and cut out small bunny ears from pink construction paper. Cut the tissue paper the same size as the paper plates.

LEARNING CIRCLE ACTIVITY

1. Using felt pens and crayons have the children draw and color designs on their eggs.
2. Have them cut out each egg.
3. When each child finishes their eggs, they choose a colored tissue paper circle. Have them glue the tissue paper onto a paper plate. This is their "grass."
4. Have them glue their eggs onto the tissue paper.
5. Now they can make their bunny! They choose a colored cotton ball and glue the bunny ears onto the cotton ball. Then they glue their bunny onto their nest.

EXPANDING KNOWLEDGE

Talk about the Easter Bunny. Why does a bunny deliver Easter eggs and not another animal? There are other animals that hop! What other animals do you think could deliver Easter eggs as fast as a bunny? If you were the Easter Bunny, how would you deliver the Easter eggs? Would you hop? Use roller skates?

MATERIALS FOR TEACHING TIPS

Chick stickers.

TEACHING TIPS

Give each child a chick sticker when they finish their nest. Have them choose an egg to stick it on. This egg will not be delivered by the Easter Bunny. It has a baby chick inside!

DINOSAUR BOX MURAL

MATERIALS

Boxes (one per child), paint, paintbrushes, rocks, green gravel, small styrofoam balls, dried weeds, glue.

PREPARATION

Gather the objects. Each child can bring a small box such as a shoebox from home.

LEARNING CIRCLE ACTIVITY

1. Assemble a part of the Box Mural each day. Talk about each part as it is added. Paint the bottom of the box blue. This is a large lake.
2. Hunt outside for rocks. Paint some of the rocks like volcanos using red paint for lava. Paint some of the rocks brown for mountains.

3. Glue the rocks on the bottom of the box.
4. Add green gravel to the box. This is the lush green plant life that existed with the dinosaurs. This gravel can be found at most pet stores.
5. Add dried weeds or moss for a dinosaur nest. These can be found at craft stores.
6. Add small styrofoam balls for dinosaur eggs.

MATERIALS FOR EXPANDING KNOWLEDGE

Sand, seaweed, driftwood, seashells, rocks, coral, tiny dried sea creatures.

EXPANDING KNOWLEDGE

Make beach boxes! Add sand, seaweed, driftwood, seashells, rocks, coral, and tiny dried sea creatures such as starfish and seahorses. If a beach is not available, a craft or shell shop can provide many of these objects.

Have each child show their finished Box Mural. Have them think of a name for the place they have designed. Would you like to live there? Why?

MATERIALS FOR TEACHING TIPS

Rubber dinosaurs, seashells.

TEACHING TIPS

Promise a special surprise at the end of each Box Mural. Save a special addition for last. Give everyone a rubber dinosaur at the end of their project. Save a special selection of shells for the beach box.

THING PAINTING

MATERIALS

White paper, paint, small objects such as feathers, rubber bands, leaves, cookie cutters, plastic forks, Q-tips, round carrot slices, flowers, paper clips, or yarn.

PREPARATION

Gather the objects.

LEARNING CIRCLE ACTIVITY

1. Give each child some paint and a sheet of paper.
2. Offer a selection of small objects.
3. Have each child make a picture by making prints with the objects or painting with them.

EXPANDING KNOWLEDGE

Show the pictures at the Learning Circle. See if the children can guess what objects made what design.

What design on each picture do you like the best?
Would you wear that design on your shirt?
Where else could you put that design? On a wall? On a bed sheet? On a dinner plate?

MATERIALS FOR TEACHING TIPS

Happy face stickers.

TEACHING TIPS

Tell the children that if they can finish their pictures without getting paint on themselves, they will get a happy face sticker.

BUILD A BIRD NEST

MATERIALS

Green playdough, paper bags, feathers, yarn, grass, leaves, twigs, rocks, cotton.

PREPARATION

Place the feathers, yarn, grass, leaves, twigs, rocks, and cotton in different parts of the classroom.

LEARNING CIRCLE ACTIVITY

1. Give each child a paper bag and some playdough.
2. Go on a bird nest hunt! Each child walks around the room and collects material to make a bird nest.
3. They come back to the Learning Circle and shape their playdough into a bird nest.
4. Have them use the materials that they found to decorate their nest.

EXPANDING KNOWLEDGE

Talk about the homes of many kinds of animals. Talk about the types of homes that people live in. Would you like to live in a bird nest? Why?

MATERIALS FOR TEACHING TIPS

Colored playdough.

TEACHING TIPS

When each child finishes a nest, they can place bird eggs in it. Offer a selection of colored playdough. Each child rolls small eggs from this and places the bird eggs in their nest.

ROCK SCULPTURES

MATERIALS

Colored posterboard, various shaped rocks, glue, scissors.

PREPARATION

Cut posterboard into large squares for each child.

LEARNING CIRCLE ACTIVITY

1. Explain what a sculptor does.
2. Tell the children that they can be sculptors and that they are going to create a design from rocks.
3. Offer a selection of rocks and a piece of posterboard to each child.
4. Have them glue the rocks on the posterboard.

EXPANDING KNOWLEDGE

Every child talks about their sculpture and explains what it is. Talk about the many uses of rocks.

What do we build out of rocks?
Where do rocks come from?
How do animals use rocks?

MATERIALS FOR TEACHING TIPS

Pictures of sculptures and statues.

TEACHING TIPS

Display various pictures of sculptures and statues while the children are creating their rock sculptures. Encourage them to become great artists. Help them to dream!

CIRCLE ART

MATERIALS

White paper, colored posterboard, felt pens, scissors.

PREPARATION

Cut a circle from the posterboard for each child.

LEARNING CIRCLE ACTIVITY

1. Give each child some paper, a circle, and felt pens.
2. They hold the circle in place and trace around it with a felt pen. Encourage them to trace the circle with different colors of felt pen.

MATERIALS FOR EXPANDING KNOWLEDGE

Pictures of modern art.

EXPANDING KNOWLEDGE

Introduce modern art by showing pictures of different forms of modern art.

Introduce the concept of interlapping where the edge of one circle is partially drawn inside another circle. Have each child try an example of interlapping on their paper. They draw two circles close together so their edges overlap. Point out the section that is a part of both circles. Color the overlap. Watch overlaps grow on their papers. Watch the excitement of being able to do something new!

MATERIALS FOR TEACHING TIPS

Stickers.

TEACHING TIPS

Place a circle sticker on the children's pictures. Tell the children that they can take their posterboard circle home. Encourage them to create circle art at home.

MARS ANIMALS

MATERIALS

Rainbow toothpicks, red posterboard, scissors, felt pens, a variety of food items such as apples, potatoes, marshmallows, grapes, raisins, carrot slices, radishes, orange and lemon peel, gum drops, and other soft candies.

PREPARATION

Cut out large red circles from the posterboard and write a child's name on each one. Cut up the food into small pieces.

LEARNING CIRCLE ACTIVITY

1. Give each child a selection of food items and toothpicks.
2. Have them create Mars Animals by connecting food items with toothpicks to make body parts and connecting bones.
3. Place each creation on a red posterboard circle. This is the red planet, Mars.

EXPANDING KNOWLEDGE

Have each child show their Mars Animals.
   What is the name of your Mars Animal?
   If life does exist on Mars, what do you
      think it would look like?
   Would they bite or would they be
      friendly?
   What color would they be?
   What would they eat?
   Would they be tiny or as big as giants?

TEACHING TIPS

Tell the children that if they do not eat their Mars Animals while they are making them, they can have some of the food for snack!

WORD ART

MATERIALS

Butcher paper, felt pens, magazines, scissors, tape.

PREPARATION

Secure a large sheet of butcher paper on a wall. Print a word such as sun, tree, eye, worm, or bug in large letters at the top of the paper. Tape a picture of the word nearby.

LEARNING CIRCLE ACTIVITY

1. Distribute felt pens to the children.
2. Invite the children to draw a picture of the word on the butcher paper using felt pens. They can continue adding pictures throughout the week.
3. Change the word often for that continued spark of interest!

MATERIALS FOR EXPANDING KNOWLEDGE

Magazines, scissors, tape.

EXPANDING KNOWLEDGE

Have the children search through magazines for pictures that match the Word Art. Have them cut out the pictures and tape them around the drawings.

Match the Word Art to the topic of study. Draw fish when learning about the ocean. Draw flowers when learning about plants.

TEACHING TIPS

Establish the rule of drawing with one color. On the day before the word changes offer rainbow drawings! Everyone can choose as many felt pens as they want.

LETTER ART

MATERIALS

Butcher paper, felt pens, scissors, magazines, tape.

PREPARATION

Secure a large sheet of butcher paper on a wall. Print an alphabet letter at the top of the paper. Tape or draw a picture near the letter that begins with that letter.

LEARNING CIRCLE ACTIVITY

1. Distribute felt pens to the children.
2. Encourage the children to use felt pens to draw the letter on the butcher paper throughout the week.
3. Change the letters as necessary.

MATERIALS FOR EXPANDING KNOWLEDGE

Magazines, scissors, tape.

EXPANDING KNOWLEDGE

Have the children search through magazines for pictures that begin with the letter that is being studied. Have them cut out the pictures and tape them on the Letter Art display.

MATERIALS FOR TEACHING TIPS

Crayons, colored chalk, paint, paintbrushes, colored pencils.

TEACHING TIPS

Explain to the children that on each day of the week they will be able to print the letter with something different. An air of mystery and anticipation adds fun to the learning experience. Offer crayons, colored chalk, paint, and colored pencils.

FUN CORNER

MATERIALS

Yarn, paper, tape, felt pens, scissors, crayons.

PREPARATION

Stretch a piece of yarn across a corner attaching the ends of the yarn to opposite walls. Tie shorter strings of yarn along this yarn so they are dangling towards the floor.

LEARNING CIRCLE ACTIVITY

1. Distribute paper, scissors, felt pens, and crayons to the children.
2. Have the children draw designs on their paper, color them, and cut them out.
3. Tape their designs on the ends of the dangling strings.
4. Call this the Fun Corner! Change the designs often.

EXPANDING KNOWLEDGE

Have the children draw spiders and ghosts to hang at Halloween. Hang Easter eggs at Easter. Hang snakes when learning the letter *S*. Hang airplanes when learning about transportation. Hang letters in a certain order to spell a child's name!

MATERIALS FOR TEACHING TIPS

Books.

TEACHING TIPS

Whenever you change designs, read a special story in the Fun Corner that relates to the designs. Read a spooky story under the ghosts! Read a rabbit story under the Easter eggs.

ROLL ART

MATERIALS

Colored construction paper, white paper, glue, scissors, felt pens.

PREPARATION

Cut construction paper in strips of different lengths.

LEARNING CIRCLE ACTIVITY

1. Give each child a sheet of white paper, strips of construction paper, and glue.
2. Everyone draws a picture such as a flower, a balloon, or a butterfly.
3. Then have everyone roll up the strips of construction paper and glue them on their pictures to enhance the design.

EXPANDING KNOWLEDGE

Discuss possible ideas for a Roll Art picture. Have each child make a suggestion. Have everyone make a different picture and share their picture at a Learning Circle. Guess what the pictures are!

When the children are learning about the letter *W*, draw a giant sheep on a piece of paper. Have everyone glue on as many rolled strips of paper as they can. You will have a rainbow sheep with thick curly wool!

TEACHING TIPS

While everyone is working on their picture, have them choose a strip of rolled paper. Print their name inside the strip. Then they glue this strip on their picture. Have everyone try to remember where their name strip is located on their picture. They can surprise their families with their hidden name.

Instead of printing their name print the word *Hi* or *Smile*!

SOCK PUPPET FANTASY

MATERIALS

Socks, glue, various small objects such as buttons, material scraps, cut up tissue paper, plastic eyes, yarn, pennies, and ribbon.

PREPARATION

Gather the small objects.

LEARNING CIRCLE ACTIVITY

1. Give each child a sock.
2. Offer each child a selection of small objects to glue on their sock to create a Sock Puppet.

EXPANDING KNOWLEDGE

After the puppets have dried, have each child wear their puppet at a Learning Circle.

Each child stands in front of the class and everyone says "hi" to their puppet. Let the children talk to each puppet. Have them name their puppets.

TEACHING TIPS

When you begin the puppet making, tell the children that they will be able to put on a puppet show when they are all finished.

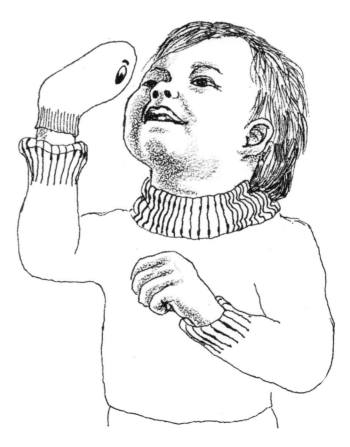

PAPER PUPPET FANTASY

MATERIALS

Paper bags, glue, various objects such as cut up pieces of construction paper, yarn, fake fur, pipe cleaners, cotton balls, sticky stars, and plastic eyes.

PREPARATION

Gather the small objects.

LEARNING CIRCLE ACTIVITY

1. Give each child a paper bag and a selection of various objects.
2. Have them glue the objects on their paper bags to create a Paper Puppet.

EXPANDING KNOWLEDGE

Have each child give their puppet a name and tell where it came from.

If the children are learning about space, make space creatures from different planets! If the topic is the ocean, make sea serpents.

MATERIALS FOR TEACHING TIPS

The story of *Pinnochio*.

TEACHING TIPS

Tell the children that you are going to read them a special story when they finish their puppets. While they hold their puppets, read them the story of *Pinnochio*.

FOIL ART

MATERIALS

Black construction paper, foil, glue, scissors.

PREPARATION

Cut the foil into large and small squares and strips.

LEARNING CIRCLE ACTIVITY

1. Give each child a sheet of construction paper and pieces of foil.
2. Have them create Foil Art by gluing the foil on the paper.
3. Demonstrate ways to shape the foil. Crunch it into balls. Roll it up. Fold a square in half, open it up, and glue the edges down with the crease up. This makes a foil mountain! Roll and twist to make a foil snake. Bend the edges of a piece up to make a foil nest. Lay the foil flat to create designs.

EXPANDING KNOWLEDGE

Have an art show. Display the pictures. Have every child talk about their design and explain what they are.

What would it be like if everything was made out of foil? What would foil beds, shoes, grass, or roads be like?

MATERIALS FOR TEACHING TIPS

Foil, pennies, balloons, erasers, small rubber balls.

TEACHING TIPS

At the end of this activity everyone chooses a foil surprise. Tightly wrap a small object such as pennies, balloons, erasers, or small rubber balls in foil. The children guess what it is by feeling it and observing its shape. Open them up!

PET ROCKS

MATERIALS

Smooth rocks, paint, paintbrushes, colored plastic eyes, different colored pipe cleaners, glue.

PREPARATION

Each child will need a rock. Cut pipe cleaners into small pieces.

LEARNING CIRCLE ACTIVITY

1. Display the rocks and materials at the Learning Circle.
2. Each child chooses a rock and paints it.
3. Each child chooses two eyes and glues them on their pet rock.
4. Bend pipe cleaners at one end.
5. The children glue on pipe cleaners for antennas.

EXPANDING KNOWLEDGE

When everyone has completed their pet rocks, place them in the middle of the Learning Circle. Ask questions about these pets.

Why would a pet rock make a nice pet?
Where is your pet rock going to sleep?
What do you think makes a pet rock happy?
What do you think would make it sad?
What is a good name for a pet rock?
Do you think your pet rock is going to get hungry?
What would a pet rock eat?

TEACHING TIPS

Sit quietly in the Learning Circle. Listen. The pet rocks are being quiet, too!

SPONGE BUILDING

MATERIALS

Green posterboard, colored sponges, scissors, glue.

PREPARATION

Cut the sponges into different shapes. Cut the posterboard into large squares, approximately eight inches by eight inches, for each child.

LEARNING CIRCLE ACTIVITY

1. Discuss what an architect does.
2. Tell the children that they can be architects.
3. The green posterboard is the grass and the sponges are the building materials.
4. Distribute the sponges and the posterboard.
5. Design a park, a shopping mall, a zoo, or a town. Glue the sponges on the poster-board to build the design.

EXPANDING KNOWLEDGE

Have every child talk about their picture and explain what they built.

Hold an imagination session! Place a sponge in the middle of the Learning Circle. Ask everyone to imagine the different things that a sponge could be. A soft shoe, a sponge car, or a pet sponge!

MATERIALS FOR TEACHING TIPS

Pictures of buildings.

TEACHING TIPS

Display various pictures of buildings while the children are working on their sponge buildings. Encourage them to build some of the structures and shapes.

BRAINSTORMS

BRAINSTORMS

Brainstorms are Learning Circle activities for the older preschool child. Interest is developed through experiments and discussions. Questions are encouraged and many possible answers are explored. At times the children may need some prompting with this method. However, listening attentively and responding positively to their answers will encourage better and better Brainstorms.

Brainstorm activities focus on the following topics: The Human Body, Nutrition, The Ocean, Land Forms, Plants, Insects, Space, The Planets, and Prehistoric Life. One topic can be used for one to two weeks. Provide plenty of time for ideas to saturate inquisitive minds. Present a limited amount of information each day. Skip a day! This will prevent tired minds and the children will anticipate new and exciting information.

Hold onto your hats, here come the Brainstorms!

THE BODY

MATERIALS

Butcher paper, felt pens, construction paper, tape, red felt material, cotton, magazines, scissors.

PREPARATION

Draw a life-sized skeleton on a sheet of butcher paper and secure it on a wall. As an option buy a skeleton frame found in many gift shops during Halloween. Draw the organs of the body on different colored construction paper. Tape them on the skeleton in their correct positions. Find magazine pages with pictures of food.

LEARNING CIRCLE ACTIVITY

1. At the Learning Circle give each child a magazine page with food pictures on it.

2. Each child cuts out a food picture and tapes it on the paper stomach. Tape food pictures traveling down the throat and esophagus!

3. Give each child a piece of red felt. Each child cuts the felt into small pieces and tapes them onto the paper lungs. This represents the tiny hairs that cover the inside of the lungs.

4. Give each child a piece of cotton. They stretch the cotton into a long thin shape and tape their piece on the small intestine, following the curves of the intestine. Now everyone can see and feel the human body!

THE HEART

MATERIALS

A large and a small orange, a bowl of water.

PREPARATION

None

LEARNING CIRCLE ACTIVITY

1. Show the children a small orange. Explain that their heart is the same size!
2. Show the children a large orange. Explain that a large orange is the same size as an adult's heart. The organs grow, too!
3. Have everyone pound their chest with their fists. When the heart beats, it pounds inside of you!

4. Tell everyone to clasp their hands together and squeeze, release, squeeze, release. This is how the heart works. When it squeezes, it pumps the blood through the body.
5. Place a bowl of water in the middle of the Learning Circle.
6. Have each child place a fist on the surface of the water and squeeze! Watch how the water squirts. This is how blood reacts when it is squeezed by the heart.

MATERIALS FOR EXPANDING KNOWLEDGE

A bowl of water, red food dye, a spoon, a cup.

EXPANDING KNOWLEDGE

Pour three quarts of water in a bowl. Dye the water red with food coloring. Let each child squirt a drop in! This is the amount of blood a child has in his or her body.

When you have a cut and you lose some blood, your body makes more! What part of your body do you think makes blood? Encourage a brainstorm of ideas, then give the answer: the inside of your bones! Have every child spoon a small amount of the red water into a cup. They have lost some blood! Pour the water back in the bowl. Your body makes more!

Have everyone flex their arms and feel their upper arm muscle. The heart is a muscle too! Run in place! Feel your heart beating faster. It is pumping blood faster to give you the energy to run. What are some other ways that you can exercise your heart?

THE BRAIN

MATERIALS

A cauliflower, gray paint, a paintbrush, a black felt pen, a knife, a lemon.

PREPARATION

Paint a medium-sized cauliflower gray. Cut a lemon in half.

LEARNING CIRCLE ACTIVITY

1. Consider the following questions. Where is your brain? What does your brain do? After soliciting answers from the children, explain that the brain controls every action that the body makes.
2. Have each child suggest an action. Blink your eyes. Wiggle your fingers. Bend your toes. The brain controls movement from your head to your toes.
3. Display the cauliflower brain. Using a black felt pen draw the different sections or rooms of the brain. Explain that different parts of the brain control different parts of the body.
4. Point to the top of the cauliflower. The top part of the brain controls the arms and legs. Move your arms and legs!
5. The lower back of the brain controls vision. Look around the room. Look at each other!
6. The side of the brain controls speech, hearing, and smell. Have each child make a noise. Did everyone hear the noises? Pass a lemon around the Learning Circle. Can you smell the lemon? Our brains are working!

MATERIALS FOR EXPANDING KNOWLEDGE

Yarn, tape.

EXPANDING KNOWLEDGE

What part of the brain controls memory? Have each child point to a room on the cauliflower brain and explain why. Use memory skills! Ask everyone to remember something that they like to eat. What is something that you don't like to eat!

Show the stem of the cauliflower. This is the brain stem. Have everyone feel the back of their neck. That is the general location of the brain stem. Tape long strings of yarn onto the cauliflower brain stem. These are the nerves in the body. They travel from the brain stem down through the bones in the back bone and into every part of the body. Have everyone feel their back bone! The nerves carry messages to and from the brain. Turn a light off and on. Explain that the electricity travels through a wire in the wall to the light. The light goes on! The brain turns on when it receives a message from a nerve. Everyone pinches their hand. The brain is receiving a message that it hurts!

Have everyone stand on one leg. When you start to lose your balance, your brain receives a message that you are falling! Your brain sends a message back to your raised leg and tells your leg to touch the ground. Your brain protects you and will not let you fall to the ground.

BONES AND MUSCLES

MATERIALS

None

PREPARATION

None

LEARNING CIRCLE ACTIVITY

1. What is your skeleton made of? Encourage responses.
2. Have everyone pretend that they do not have a skeleton. Flop down on the floor. It is impossible to sit up straight!
3. If you did not have a skeleton, what would you be? Give the children clues to help them answer the question. Answers might be a worm, a caterpillar, a jellyfish, a shark, an earlobe, or the tip of a nose!

4. Bones cannot move by themselves. Muscles move the bones. Bend your leg, move your wrist, raise your arm up and down, move your head back and forth, and stand as still as a statue. Muscles make these movements possible.
5. Have everyone smile, wrinkle their nose, or make a funny face. Muscles are in the face! Move your eyes back and forth. Open and close your eyes. Muscles control the eyes and eyelids.

EXPANDING KNOWLEDGE

Bones give you a special shape. Your bones give you a human shape. Have everyone name an animal that has a different shape than a human.

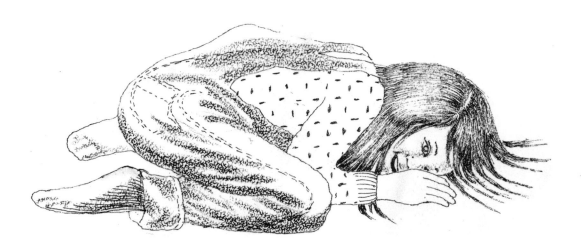

THE JOINTS

MATERIALS

Small oranges, spoons.

PREPARATION

None

LEARNING CIRCLE ACTIVITY

1. Give each child a small orange to hold. Have everyone notice how their fingers bend around the orange. Can you see the three parts of your fingers? The bones in the fingers are connected by joints. Without joints the fingers would be stiff.
2. While holding the orange have everyone stiffen their fingers. Did the orange drop?
3. What else would be hard to do if your fingers were stiff?
4. Have everyone try to walk without bending their knees. There is a joint in the knee.
5. Give everyone a spoon and then pretend to eat cereal. Now pretend to eat cereal with a stiff arm. A joint at the elbow allows the arm to bend.
6. Put the spoon on the floor. Stand up, bend at the waist, and pick up the spoon. Try to pick up the spoon without bending! There is a joint in the back that makes bending possible.
7. Have everyone place their finger on their face in front of their ear. Say the sentence "The big, bad wolf ate bananas!" There is a joint there that makes it possible to move the jaw.
8. If you could not move your mouth, what would be hard to do? Encourage a Brainstorm of ideas.

THE STOMACH

MATERIALS

Paper cups, marshmallows.

PREPARATION

None

LEARNING CIRCLE ACTIVITY

1. Solicit answers from the children before giving the correct answer. How does the food that you eat reach your stomach? Explain that it starts with the mouth!
2. Have each child spit into a paper cup.
3. Why is there saliva in your mouth? Explain that it mixes with food and moistens it. This helps the food slide down the throat.
4. Why do you have a tongue? Have everyone try to talk without moving their tongues! It also pushes food to the back of the throat.
5. Ask everyone to swallow. The muscles in the throat push the food down the esophagus. Everyone points to their esophagus.
6. Have everyone chew and swallow a marshmallow. With their finger, have everyone follow the marshmallow down the esophagus to the stomach.

MATERIALS FOR EXPANDING KNOWLEDGE

A hamburger, french fries, milk, a blender, water.

EXPANDING KNOWLEDGE

Demonstrate what happens to food when it reaches the stomach. Drop a hamburger, french fries, and milk into a blender. Add some water. This is the stomach juice that mixes with the food. Turn the blender on. This is what happens to lunch!

TINA AND GINA MURAL

MATERIALS

Butcher paper, felt pens, crayons, tape, scissors, construction paper, magazines.

PREPARATION

Trace two children on a sheet of butcher paper drawing their faces and clothing. Tape them on a wall. Draw and cut out two large lunch pails from construction paper. Tape a lunch pail on the hand of each girl. Label the girls *Tina* and *Gina*.

LEARNING CIRCLE ACTIVITY

1. Have the children color the two paper girls.
2. Discuss the eating habits of each paper girl. Tina eats food that is good for her. Solicit a Brainstorm of good food ideas.
3. Gina does not care what she eats! Ask for a Brainstorm of food ideas that are not good for the body.
4. Have the children look through magazines and cut out food pictures.
5. The children tape good food ideas on *Tina's* lunch pail and poor food ideas on *Gina's* lunch pail.

EXPANDING KNOWLEDGE

Encourage the children to bring food labels and small food items from home to tape near the paper girls. When a new food item is added, ask the children to choose the correct lunch pail for the food item. Suggested food items are small milk cartons, chewing gum, a sugar cube, a salt package, juice cans, and a small package of nuts.

GAS PUMP GAME

MATERIALS

White posterboard, felt pens, a sponge, a rope, scissors, tape.

PREPARATION

Draw a large gas pump on a posterboard. Tape the end of a short rope to one side of the pump. Cut a small sponge in half and tape both pieces on the gas pump. Label one piece *On* and the other piece *Off*. These are the *On* and *Off* buttons of the gas pump.

LEARNING CIRCLE ACTIVITY

1. Discuss how the body is like a car that is in good condition. If a car gets good fuel, it will run better. The body needs good fuel, or good food, so it can be strong and healthy.

2. Have a child stand by the gas pump and form a loose fist.

3. Put the end of the rope inside the child's fist and ask, "What can I fill you up with today?" The child pushes the *On* button. Encourage the child to answer with good food ideas.

4. If a poor food idea is mentioned, remove the rope and have the child push the *Off* button. This turns the gas pump off! Continue until everyone has had a turn.

HAPPY AND SAD POSTER

MATERIALS

Two white posterboards, felt pens, magazines, scissors, white paper, tape, paper bags.

PREPARATION

Draw a large happy face on one posterboard and a large frowning face on the other posterboard. Cut out wide slits for the mouths and tape a paper bag behind each slit.

LEARNING CIRCLE ACTIVITY

1. The children cut out food pictures from magazines or draw food pictures on white paper.
2. Have the children feed the happy face good food pictures and the sad face food pictures that are not good for you.

EXPANDING KNOWLEDGE

Why is the happy face smiling? Solicit a Brainstorm of answers. Help the children think of possible answers. Some are:

Eating good food gives you good eyesight.
It gives you healthy skin and hair.
It helps your body to grow taller.
You grow stronger and have more energy.
You can think better and your memory improves.
Your bones and teeth become stronger.
Your cuts will heal faster and nosebleeds will disappear quickly.
You will fight off colds and illnesses better.
Your heart will function better.
You will live longer!

THE RABBIT GARDEN

MATERIALS

Green posterboard, white posterboard, colored cotton balls, glue, scissors, tape.

PREPARATION

Draw pairs of rabbit ears all over the green posterboard. These are rabbits hiding in a vegetable garden! Cut two inch circles from white posterboard and glue a colored cotton ball in the middle of each circle. Print a Brainstorm question (see below) on the back of each circle and tape the circles below each pair of rabbit ears. At the Learning Circle attach the circles and tell everyone that now they can see the whole rabbit! Brainstorm questions can include:

What is your favorite dinner?

If you could plant a fruit tree in your bedroom, what kind of fruit would it bear for a late night snack?

If you could turn a glass of milk into any flavor, what would it be?

What is your favorite dessert? Would it be good for you to eat it three times a day?

If you could make a picnic basket appear in the Learning Circle, what would you like to find in it?

What is your favorite ice cream flavor? What is in ice cream that is good for you?

What could you put on a pizza that would be good for you?

What are the food items in a hamburger that are good for you?

If you could put anything in a sandwich, what would it be?

What is something good for you that you could put on a cracker?

If you woke up in the morning and you had turned into a vegetable, what would it be?

If food appeared in your mouth this very moment, what would you like it to be?

LEARNING CIRCLE ACTIVITY

1. Each child chooses a rabbit tail and answers the Brainstorm question on the back of it.
2. Tell them to choose a rabbit before it hides again in the vegetable garden!
3. Every child can take their rabbit home to share the question with their families.

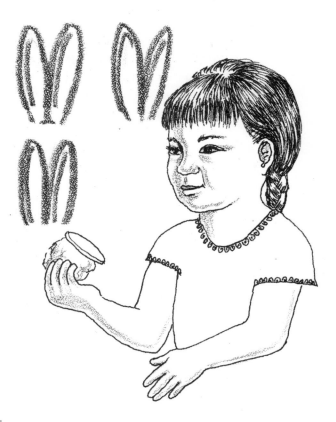

OCEAN MURAL

MATERIALS

Butcher paper, tape, felt pens, crayons, paper plates, crepe paper, white construction paper, a stapler, scissors, sponges, sticky stars, styrofoam balls, paint, paintbrushes.

PREPARATION

Secure a large sheet of butcher paper on a wall. Draw a whale six feet long on the butcher paper.

LEARNING CIRCLE ACTIVITY

1. Have the children color the whale and surrounding ocean.
2. Add jellyfish! The children color paper plates and cut streamers of crepe paper. Staple the streamers on the bottom edge of the paper plates. The children tape their jellyfish on the Mural.
3. Add electric eels. Everyone colors a sheet of white construction paper and rolls it up with the colored side out. Secure the edge with tape and draw eyes on one end of the roll. Add the eels to the Mural!
4. Add seaweed. The children cut different lengths of crepe paper and tape the streamers on the Mural.
5. Add sea sponges. The children cut up sponges and tape them on the Mural.
6. Add starfish. The children place large sticky stars on the Mural.
7. Add crabs. Paint styrofoam balls and tape them on the Mural. Draw the legs of the crabs directly on the butcher paper.

8. Draw seahorses, octopi, and sea cucumbers (shaped like cucumbers!) on white construction paper and cut them out. The children color them and tape them on the Mural.

EXPANDING KNOWLEDGE

Ask the children if they can see the whale behind the added sea-life! Count how many kinds of sea-life are on the Mural. Which sea creature would you like to be?

Learn about the different kinds of sea-life as they are added to the Mural. Add one a day!

OCEAN COLORS

MATERIALS

Water, a clear drinking glass, a mirror, colored construction paper.

PREPARATION

None

LEARNING CIRCLE ACTIVITY

1. What color is the ocean? Solicit answers from the children.
2. Place a glass of water in the middle of the Learning Circle and observe the color. If possible display a glass of ocean water!
3. Notice that the water appears clear.
4. Why does the ocean often appear blue, or green, or gray? Again, solicit responses.
5. Explain that the ocean reflects the color of the sky and the color of plant life beneath it.
6. Place a mirror on the floor in the Learning Circle. The ocean is like a giant mirror!
7. Have each child, in turn, hold a colored sheet of construction paper over the mirror. The paper is the sky.
8. Notice how the mirror looks pink when a pink sheet of paper is held over it. The mirror reflects all the different colors.
9. What colors could the ocean reflect during a sunset?
10. What color would the ocean look like during a rain storm?

EXPANDING KNOWLEDGE

How do we use the ocean? Discuss the possibilities. We can swim, water ski, surf, scuba dive, take boat rides, go fishing, and play by its beaches!

THE TIDE

MATERIALS

A rectangular pan, sand, water, material, scissors.

PREPARATION

Put an inch of sand in one half of the pan. Slowly pour an inch of water into the other half of the pan. (Hint: mix the sand with some dirt to help it stay in place.) Cut the material into small rectangle shapes.

LEARNING CIRCLE ACTIVITY

1. Place the pan in the middle of the Learning Circle. Slowly tilt the pan so that the water begins to move onto the sand. This is the ocean moving higher onto the beach. This is called high tide.
2. Tilt the pan in the opposite direction. The ocean flows away from the beach. This is called low tide.
3. Explain that the tide is the rise and fall of the surface of the ocean. It does this two times a day!
4. When it is high tide, where should your beach towel be?
5. Give each child a piece of material shaped like a beach towel. Have each child, in turn, place their beach towel on a part of the sand where they think it should go.

6. When it is low tide, where could you walk without getting your feet wet? Have each child, in turn, walk on the sand using their fingers to show where they would walk.

EXPANDING KNOWLEDGE

What makes the ocean rise and fall? After the children answer, explain that the Moon pulls on the Earth. When this happens, the ocean level rises. Have everyone in the Learning Circle stand up and raise their arms upward. When the Moon's pull is not as strong, the level of the ocean falls. Have everyone slowly sit back down in the Learning Circle.

SALT WATER

MATERIALS

Water, a clear drinking glass, salt, a raw egg.

PREPARATION

Fill the glass half full with water.

LEARNING CIRCLE ACTIVITY

1. Can we drink ocean water? Invite responses.
2. Demonstrate the effect of salt in water. Fill a glass half full with water.
3. Place a raw egg in the water.
4. Watch the egg sink to the bottom of the glass.
5. Pour salt into the water until the egg rises to the surface.
6. Explain that a large amount of salt in the water will cause objects to float.
7. Have each child put a small drop of salt water on their tongue. How does it taste?

GOLDFISH

MATERIALS

A goldfish, a bowl of water, a balloon.

PREPARATION

None

LEARNING CIRCLE ACTIVITY

1. Observe a goldfish at the Learning Circle.
2. Consider the following questions. Why does the fish move its tail and fins? (The fins and tail help the fish move in different directions.)
3. What happens if the fish moves its tail and fins very fast? (It swims very fast!)
4. What is a gill? (It is an organ on the side of its body that allows the fish to breathe.)
5. What organ helps you to breathe? (The lungs.)
6. What does a fish breathe? (The air in the water.)
7. What do you breathe? (Air!)
8. How does a fish swim to the top of the bowl or the bottom of the bowl? (It uses an organ called a bladder.)
9. Blow up a balloon and call it a bladder. When the fish inflates its bladder, it rises.
10. Let some of the air out of the balloon. When the fish deflates its bladder, it sinks to the bottom.

FISH BRAINSTORMS

MATERIALS

Butcher paper, crayons, colored construction paper, scissors, a felt pen, paper clips, yarn, a stick, a magnet.

PREPARATION

Place a large sheet of butcher paper on the floor. This is the ocean. Have the children color the ocean. Cut out fish shapes from different colors of construction paper. Attach a paper clip to each fish and place them on the butcher paper. Tie a string of yarn onto a stick. Attach a magnet onto the other end of the yarn. Print Brainstorm questions on the back of the fish. Brainstorm questions can include:

If you were a fish, how big would you want to be?

What color would you like to be, if you were a fish?

If you were a fish, where would you hide if you saw a hungry shark?

Does it sound like fun to be a fish? Why?

If you turned into a fish, what would you miss most about living on dry land?

What are some good things about being a fish in a fishbowl instead of the ocean?

Would you rather be a whale, an octopus, or a shark? Why?

If a fish could talk, what do you think it would tell you about the ocean.

If you were a fish, what would frighten you?

What kind of noise would you like to make if you were a fish?

LEARNING CIRCLE ACTIVITY

1. Each child, in turn, aims the fishing pole at a fish.
2. They answer the question on the back of the fish that they caught.
3. They can take their fish home to share the fish question with their families.

MOUNTAINS

MATERIALS

Colored construction paper.

PREPARATION

None

LEARNING CIRCLE ACTIVITY

1. Make mountains! Explain that mountains are formed by movement inside the Earth causing the land to push upward.
2. The children each choose a color of construction paper. Offer brown for a mountain covered with dirt; white for a snow covered mountain; green for a mountain covered with trees; and blue for a mountain with many lakes.
3. The children lay their papers on the floor.
4. Have them place their hands flat on each short side of the paper.
5. Everyone slowly pushes their hands together. The paper will bend upward to form a mountain.

MATERIALS FOR EXPANDING KNOWLEDGE

Crayons, scissors, white posterboard, white paper, felt pens.

EXPANDING KNOWLEDGE

Draw a large mountain on the posterboard and color it. Lay it down flat in the middle of the Learning Circle. Draw stick figures on white paper with felt pens and print a child's name by each one. Cut them out and print a mountain Brainstorm question on the back of each figure. Place them at the base of the mountain. Every child finds the stick figure with their name on it, and, in turn, answers the question on the back. They can then place their "mountain climber" anywhere on the mountain! Mountain Brainstorm questions can include:

Do you look up or down to see a mountain?

Is a mountain bigger at the top or at the bottom? (The bottom or base of a mountain is always bigger. Look at a triangle shape!)

What do you think is inside a mountain?

If you climbed to the top of a mountain, what do you think you would see?

What kind of animals live on mountains?

Would it be fun to live on a mountain? Why?

What would be a good name for a very tall mountain?

What would be a good name for a very small mountain?

Why do you think people climb mountains?

How do we use mountains? (We build roads, tunnels, and bridges on them, or observatories to study the stars. We grow food on them, ski down them, fish in their lakes, and hike on them!)

ISLANDS

MATERIALS

A large pan, water, blue food coloring, two large rocks, paint, a paintbrush, five smaller rocks, sponges, flower seeds, small plastic animals, rubber bands, small leaves, small twigs.

PREPARATION

Paint one of the large rocks black and the other large rock green. Fill a pan half full of water and dye the water blue. Place the large black rock in the middle of the pan. Place the smaller rocks in the water so that none of the rocks are touching. Place the large green rock near the pan on the floor. Learn the story.

LEARNING CIRCLE ACTIVITY

1. Explain that the rocks are land and the water is the ocean. Notice that the water completely surrounds the rocks. This makes them islands!
2. Distribute sponges, flower seeds, small leaves, twigs, rubber bands, and small plastic animals to the children.
3. How is an island made? After listening to the responses, tell a story that describes the formation of an island. A suggested story:

Under the ocean, a volcano erupted! Hot lava shot up through the ocean and hit the surface. It cooled and hardened forming a large shiny black rock. (Point to the black rock in the pan. This is the cooled lava.) Over a long period of time wind and rain beat against the rock and broke its surface into many small pieces. (Have the children blow on the rock. For the rain, the children can squeeze a damp sponge over the rock.) Dirt now covered the rock. Waves beat against the rock and ground the pieces into sand. (For the waves, everyone can gently push the water with their hands so that it hits the rock.) Eventually, plants, insects, and animals came to live on the island. The wind carried flower and grass seeds to the island. (Have the children sprinkle flower seeds on the rock.) Small insects were carried by the wind. Coconuts were brought by the waves. They grew into palm trees. Tiny animals such as ants and snails rode to the island on large palm leaves. (Have each child place a leaf in the water.) Lizards, snakes, and worms drifted to the island on floating tree branches. (Have each child place a twig in the water and a rubber band on the rock for a snake!) People eventually came by boat and brought animals with them. (Have each child place a plastic animal on the rock.)

ICEBERGS

MATERIALS

Bowls, water, ice cubes, a picture of an iceberg.

PREPARATION

Make ice cubes. Fill a bowl half full of water for each child.

LEARNING CIRCLE ACTIVITY

1. Show a picture of an iceberg. What do you think an iceberg is made of?
2. After hearing the responses explain that an iceberg is like a giant ice cube floating in the ocean.
3. Give each child a bowl of water and an ice cube.
4. Have everyone drop their ice cube into their bowl. Does it sink or float? Explain that ice is lighter then water.
5. Notice that most of the ice cube is under the water. This is the way an iceberg floats in the water. Only the top of the iceberg shows!

MATERIALS FOR EXPANDING KNOWLEDGE

Small objects such as rocks, marbles, a sponge cut into small pieces, leaves.

EXPANDING KNOWLEDGE

Drop a variety of small objects into the water and discover which ones are lighter or heavier than water.

GLACIERS

MATERIALS

A pan, a hammer, water, white paper, bowls, hot water, a tray.

PREPARATION

Freeze a pan of water. Fill a bowl half full of water for each child.

LEARNING CIRCLE ACTIVITY

1. Where do icebergs come from? After listening to the responses explain that they come from a much larger mass of ice called a glacier.
2. Explain that a glacier is made of snow. As snow piles up higher and higher each year, the pressure on the bottom layer of snow is so great that it changes into ice!
3. Place a sheet of white paper on the floor and add five sheets, one at a time, on top of it. Each sheet is a snowfall. The bottom sheet changes into ice.
4. The glacier becomes a large river of ice slowly moving downhill. Place the sheets of paper in a long row. A glacier can be as long as a street or a town! When a part of the glacier breaks off into the sea, it becomes an iceberg.
5. Run hot water over the frozen pan of water to loosen it.
6. Invert it onto a tray. This is a glacier!
7. Using a hammer break off chunks of ice to form icebergs. (Have the children place their hands over their eyes for protection.)
8. The children float the ice in their bowls.

CAVES

MATERIALS

A bed sheet, a flashlight, a jar, water.

PREPARATION

Hang a bed sheet so that it resembles a cave. Fill a jar half full of water. Learn the cave questions.

LEARNING CIRCLE ACTIVITY

1. Explain that a cave is an underground hole formed by the Earth. If the class went outside and dug a hole or an animal dug a hole, it would not be a true cave!

2. What is it like inside a cave? Find out! Have everyone crawl inside the hanging bed sheet. Turn on a flashlight while crawling in.

3. While sitting in the cave, create a Brainstorm with the following cave questions:

   Is it dark or light inside a cave? (Have everyone close their eyes. It is that dark in a cave.)

   Why is it so dark in a cave?

   How do you think the air smells in a cave? (It smells fresh and clean.)

   Why do you think the air has stayed so clean?

   Is it quiet or noisy in a cave? (The only sound you might hear is dripping water. Slowly shake the jar of water!)

   What sounds won't you be able to hear?

   What animals live in a cave? (Bats, birds, insects, frogs, worms, snails, and fish.)

Some cave animals do not have eyes! What other senses can they use?

Would you like to live in a cave? Why?

If you were a cave explorer, what are some cave rules that you should follow? (Bring a flashlight; use chalk to mark your course so you won't get lost; bring a rope, water, a snack, and a first aid kit; and wear the right kind of clothing such as jeans, boots, a jacket, gloves, a backpack, and a hard hat.)

DISCOVERY GARDEN MURAL

MATERIALS

Butcher paper, tape, felt pens, crayons.

PREPARATION

Secure a large sheet of butcher paper on a wall.

LEARNING CIRCLE ACTIVITY

1. Explain that when someone discovers a new plant, tree, or flower, they give it a name.

2. Give the children a selection of felt pens and crayons.
3. Everyone draws and colors plants, flowers, and trees on the Mural.
4. Ask the children to draw a new type of plant life that they would like to discover.
5. Print the name of each child by a plant, flower, or tree that they have drawn.
6. At the Learning Circle every child can think of a name for their new plant.

MATERIALS FOR EXPANDING KNOWLEDGE

Paper plates, felt material, colored cotton balls, rubber bands, scissors, tape.

EXPANDING KNOWLEDGE

Offer a variety of materials to make plant life. The children can color paper plates for flower heads and tape them on the Mural. Offer colorful felt circles and colored cotton balls for flower heads and tree blossoms. Tape colorful rubber bands on a tree for a rubber band tree!

PLANT BRAINSTORMS

MATERIALS

White posterboard, felt pens, crayons, two large plastic eyes, glue.

PREPARATION

Draw a large plant on the posterboard and color it. Glue two plastic eyes on the plant. Display it at the Learning Circle. Learn the Plant Brainstorm questions.

LEARNING CIRCLE ACTIVITY

1. To help the children learn about plants and gain an appreciation for them, invite a Brainstorm with the following questions. If necessary, help the children to think of possible answers.

   Where do plants grow? (Oceans, lakes, deserts, mountains, gardens, on rocks, on wood, and in snow!)

   How can we tell that plants are alive? (We can watch them grow! Vines twist and turn their stems. They grow towards the sun. Buds open into flowers. They fight for ground space! Weeds can over take a garden.)

   What kind of food do plants make? (Potatoes, carrots, beets, cucumbers, watermelons, strawberries.)

   What happens to a plant when you pull it from the ground? (It will die unless you put it into a pot with soil and water.)

   How can we keep a plant healthy? (Give the plant the right amount of water, sunshine, and food. Be gentle when touching a plant. Spray the plant with bug spray if insects are harming it.)

CARNATION CREATIONS

MATERIALS

White carnations, food coloring, clear drinking glasses.

PREPARATION

Fill the glasses with water, one for each child.

LEARNING CIRCLE ACTIVITY

1. Give each child a white carnation and have them place it in a glass.
2. Each child can choose a colored food dye to drop into the water.
3. Discuss the effect the colored water will have on the flower, and why.
4. Observe the flowers each morning and notice the change in color.
5. After the flowers have turned different colors, every child can think of a new name for their flower.

EXPANDING KNOWLEDGE

If you could make many flowers, what would you do with them? Possible answers are to grow them in gardens, to use them as hair decorations or to decorate floats, to string them for necklaces, to use them as a scent for perfume, to make flower arrangements, or to press them under glass.

EXAMINE A LEAF

MATERIALS

Leaves.

PREPARATION

Collect similar leaves, one for each child.
Learn the leaf questions.

LEARNING CIRCLE ACTIVITY

1. Give each child a leaf to hold.
2. Create a Brainstorm with the following
   questions about the leaf.
   What color is the leaf?
   Is the leaf thick or thin?

Can you see sunshine through the leaf?
(A leaf is thin so that the sunshine
can reach all parts of the leaf.)
Does the leaf feel smooth or rough?
(Most leaves are smooth and waxy to
keep the moisture in and prevent
them from drying out.)
Can you see lines on the leaf? (These
are veins that strengthen the leaf.)

EXAMINE A FLOWER

MATERIALS

Flowers.

PREPARATION

Collect different kinds of flowers, one for
each child. Learn the flower questions.

LEARNING CIRCLE ACTIVITY

1. Give each child a flower to hold.
2. The following questions about the flowers

will encourage a Brainstorm of answers.
What color is the flower?
Where is the stem of the flower?
Where are the petals?
What is the shape of the petals?
What does the flower smell like?
Why do you think people like flowers?

FLOWER PETAL GAME

MATERIALS

Blue posterboard, black felt pens, colored construction paper, tape, scissors.

PREPARATION

Draw a large flower head on a blue poster-board. Cut out petals from colored construction paper. Print a flower question on the back of each petal and tape them around the flower head. Suggested flower petal questions are listed below.

What color would you be?

What kind of insect would you like to attract?

What would you smell like—chocolate, perfume, or french fries?

How tall would you be?

If someone picked you, what would you say to them?

If someone picked you, where would you like to go—in a vase, in someone's hair, or in a fish tank?

Where would you like to grow—in a garden, on a mountain, or at the bottom of the ocean?

What would you be afraid of—someone stepping on you, a lawn mower, or a rabbit nibbling on your petals?

What kind of flower would you be?

If someone in the Learning Circle could pick you and take you home, who would it be?

LEARNING CIRCLE ACTIVITY

1. Tell the children to imagine that they are flowers. Each child, in turn, chooses a petal and answers the flower petal question.

2. The children can take their petals home and share the question with their families.

EXPANDING KNOWLEDGE

Call a plant talk session! Place a plant in the middle of the Learning Circle. Discuss the idea that plants may be affected by a person's attitude towards them. Have everyone say one nice thing to the plant. Encourage a kind and caring feeling towards plants.

THE ANT

MATERIALS

White posterboard, felt pens.

PREPARATION

Draw a large ant on a posterboard.

LEARNING CIRCLE ACTIVITY

1. Display the posterboard ant. Explain that an insect like an ant has three body parts - the head, the middle, and the lower body.
2. Count the different body parts on the ant.
3. Explain that humans have two body parts - the upper body above the waist and the lower body below the waist.
4. Have a child stand in front of the Learning Circle. Show the upper and lower body of this child.
5. Count the body parts! Are three body parts more than two body parts?
6. Count the legs of the ant. Have everyone count their legs. What would it be like to have six legs?
7. Does the ant have ears? Have everyone point to their ears. Where is the nose on the ant? Everyone points to their nose. Explain that an ant does not have ears or a nose! The ant has two antennae that feel and smell. Do humans have antennae?

EXPANDING KNOWLEDGE

Explain that most insects have wings. What do you have that you can flap like wings? Why would it be fun to have wings? Listen to the responses.

When an insect is frightened, it will bite, sting, or emit a poisonous spray. If you were a frightened insect, which would you do? What do you do when you are frightened?

THE ANT NEST

MATERIALS

Butcher paper, felt pens, crayons, lollipops, food labels, tape, scissors, magazines, a green sponge, red construction paper.

PREPARATION

Draw a large ant nest on a sheet of butcher paper, approximately six feet by three feet, and secure it on a wall. Draw many connecting tunnels and rooms. Label the rooms queen room, larva room, cocoon room, trash room, food room, garden room, and winged ant room. Draw twenty ants, approximately eight inches long, from red construction paper and cut them out. Draw one of the ants larger then the rest to make the queen ant.

LEARNING CIRCLE ACTIVITY

1. Have the children color the ant nest.
2. Have them draw round circles in the queen's room for eggs.
3. Have them draw ovals in the larva room and striped ovals in the cocoon room.
4. Cut food pictures from magazines and tape them in the food room.
5. Have each child tape a lollipop or food label in the trash room. This is the room where food is left to be thrown away.
6. Have each child cut off a piece from a green sponge and tape it in the garden room. This is the fungus that the ants grow for food.
7. Have the children tape the ants in the tunnels and rooms.
8. Draw wings on the ants in the winged ant room.
9. The teacher tapes the queen ant in the queen room!
10. Discuss the life of an ant nest. Refer to the mural many times during the discussion.

MATERIALS FOR EXPANDING KNOWLEDGE

White construction paper, tape, felt pens, crayons.

EXPANDING KNOWLEDGE

Draw six ants on white construction paper and secure on a wall. What color is an ant? Each child names a color. When a child says a correct color of an ant, this child colors one of the ants that color. Ants come in red, black, brown, blue, yellow, and green!

   If you were an ant, what would you be afraid of? Have the children Brainstorm the question. Possible answers are cars, bicycles, weather, lizards, frogs, anteaters, someone stepping on you, or other ants from different ant nests.

BEEHIVE MURAL

MATERIALS

Butcher paper, felt pens, crayons, white construction paper, scissors, tape.

PREPARATION

Secure a large sheet of butcher paper on a wall. Fill the paper with large hexagon shapes grouped like a beehive. In some of the cells draw baby bees shaped like large kidney beans. Draw large bees from white construction paper and cut them out. Make the bees approximately eight inches long.

LEARNING CIRCLE ACTIVITY

1. Have the children draw circles in some of the cells for pollen.
2. Have them color some of the cells gold for honey.
3. Have them draw baby bees!
4. Everyone can color the cells of the beehive.
5. The children then color the paper bees and tape them on the beehive.
6. Discuss the activities of a beehive!

EXPANDING KNOWLEDGE

Invite a Brainstorm with these questions about bees. Tell the children to imagine that they are bees.

What color flower would attract you?
Where would you like to build your hive?
Would you enjoy your life? Why?
If you were caught in a rainstorm, where would you hide?
If you could make something besides honey, what would it be?
What two colors would you like to be, instead of black and orange?
What would make you angry enough to sting somebody?
What would your name be?
If a bear tried to take your honey, what would you say to the bear?
If you could make a noise other then buzz, what would it be?

ANT IMAGINATION

MATERIALS

Butcher paper, felt pens, tape.

PREPARATION

Draw a giant flower on a long sheet of butcher paper, approximately eight feet tall! Secure this on a wall.

LEARNING CIRCLE ACTIVITY

1. The children lay under the flower on their backs.
2. Imagine how flowers must look to an ant!
3. What else would look large to an ant? Brainstorm the question.

MATERIALS FOR EXPANDING KNOWLEDGE

White posterboard, felt pens, scissors, tape.

EXPANDING KNOWLEDGE

Play a memory game! Draw two inch circles on white posterboard and cut them out. Draw an ant in each circle and color them red, black, brown, blue, yellow, and green. Draw a large mound of dirt on a white posterboard and tape the ants on the mound. If you were an ant, which color would you like to be? Have each child choose a colored ant from the mound, place the ant in their hand, and try to remember one thing that they have learned about ants. After everyone has had a turn, they can take their ant home!

THE MILKY WAY GALAXY

MATERIALS

White posterboard, red, yellow, and blue felt pens, a *Milky Way* candy bar, tape.

PREPARATION

Using the felt pens draw numerous dots in a spiral shape on the posterboard. The dots are stars. This represents the Milky Way Galaxy.

LEARNING CIRCLE ACTIVITY

1. What is a star? Talk about stars being a ball of light!
2. Let each child choose a red, yellow, or blue felt pen and add a group of stars to the poster. Explain that stars are red, yellow, blue, or white.
3. As the children watch, draw nine large dots within the spiral. These are the nine Planets. Have the children count the Planets. Draw an arrow pointing to the Earth.
4. Draw a yellow dot larger then the planets. This is the Sun. It is a yellow star!
5. Point to all the stars. Tell the children that this group of stars is called the Milky Way Galaxy. This consists of the Sun, the nine Planets and a large group of stars.
6. Cut a *Milky Way* candy bar into small pieces and give everyone a taste.
7. Secure the *Milky Way* wrapper on the posterboard. Display this poster while learning about space. Keep new thoughts visible!

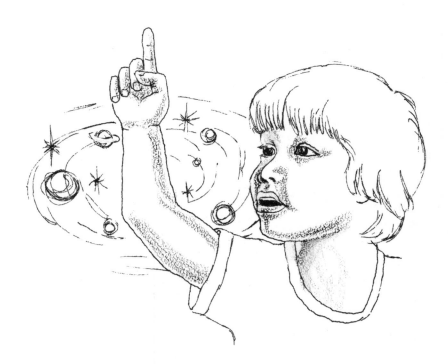

THE SUN

MATERIALS

Yellow posterboard, blue felt pen, gold sticky stars.

PREPARATION

Draw a large circle on the posterboard. This is the Sun.

LEARNING CIRCLE ACTIVITY

1. Draw a tiny blue dot on the yellow Sun. This is the Earth!
2. Which is bigger, the Sun or the Earth?
3. Talk about the size of the Sun and that it is a yellow star.
4. Have each child place a gold sticky star on the Sun. As every child does this, they complete the sentence, "The sun is bigger than a _____!" (a whale, a dinosaur, a Planet!)

MATERIALS FOR EXPANDING KNOWLEDGE

A yellow balloon.

EXPANDING KNOWLEDGE

Why does the sun look so big and the other stars in the sky look so small? Blow up a yellow balloon to three inches in diameter. Stand twenty feet from the children and walk slowly towards them while blowing up the balloon to ten inches in diameter. The Sun looks bigger because it is closer to us than all the other stars!

THE EARTH

MATERIALS

A yellow balloon, pictures of animals, a glass of water, a large rock.

PREPARATION

Blow up the balloon.

LEARNING CIRCLE ACTIVITY

1. Why is the Earth different from the other planets? Encourage a Brainstorm of answers.
2. Display three objects - the yellow balloon for the Sun, a glass of water, and pictures of animals. The Earth is the only planet that has the right amount of Sun, a source of water, and life.
3. Display a large rock. Explain that the Earth is a ball of rock. It is solid and can be touched. Pound the floor! Jump on the floor!

MATERIALS FOR EXPANDING KNOWLEDGE

A yellow balloon, a blue balloon, picture of a child, tape.

EXPANDING KNOWLEDGE

Discuss the movement of the Earth. Have a child hold the yellow balloon for the sun. Have another child hold the blue balloon for the Earth. Tape a picture of a child on the blue balloon. Have the child holding the blue balloon walk around the Sun. The child turns the blue balloon as he or she walks. When the child on the balloon faces the Sun, it is day. When the child turns away from the Sun, it is night. The Earth moves, not the Sun!

Have everyone look out a window. Is it day or night? Is the class facing the Sun?

GRAVITY

MATERIALS

A rope, various objects such as cotton balls, balloons, feathers, small rubber balls, and colored construction paper.

PREPARATION

Blow up the balloons. Crunch up sheets of construction paper to make paper balls.

LEARNING CIRCLE ACTIVITY

1. Explain that the Earth pulls everything towards it. This pull is called gravity.
2. Stand at one end of a rope. Have each child, in turn, stand at the other end of the rope.
3. Pull on the rope while each child holds it. Let each child experience the feeling of being pulled!
4. Have the children throw various objects in the air such as cotton balls, balloons, feathers, small rubber balls, or wads of construction paper. Notice how fast or slow each object falls towards the Earth.
5. Count how many times a rubber ball bounces on the floor. How many times did gravity pull it down?

MATERIALS FOR EXPANDING KNOWLEDGE

A sock, a shoe, a heavy book, a pencil, a straw, a spoon.

EXPANDING KNOWLEDGE

Explain that gravity pulls harder on objects that are heavier. Display three objects - a sock, a shoe, and a heavy book. Lift the objects. Which object is the lightest? Which object is the heaviest? Which object does gravity pull the hardest on?

Explain that gravity pulls the hardest on the center of an object. Find the center of various objects. Balance a pencil, a straw, and a spoon using just a finger. The part of the pencil, straw, or spoon that is touching the finger is the center of the object. What else could be balanced on a finger?

VENUS

MATERIALS

A bowl of water, yellow food dye, pans, spoons, a flashlight.

PREPARATION

None

LEARNING CIRCLE ACTIVITY

1. Explain that Venus is covered with yellow clouds.
2. Drop yellow food dye into a bowl of water. Watch the yellow swirls in the water like clouds moving across a sky.
3. Explain that thunder and lightening surround the surface of Venus.
4. Give each child a pan and a spoon.
5. Show the children the flashlight. Turn the flashlight on and off while every child bangs on their pan with their spoon to make thunder. Experience Venus!

MATERIALS FOR EXPANDING KNOWLEDGE

Different sizes of styrofoam balls.

EXPANDING KNOWLEDGE

Explain that Venus and Earth are so close in size that they are called the twin planets. Place various sizes of styrofoam balls in a straight line. Who can find the styrofoam balls that are almost the same size? See who can find the smallest ball. Which one is the largest?

SATURN

MATERIALS

A picture of Saturn, ice, a hammer, small and large rocks, a pan, paper bags.

PREPARATION

Crush the ice with a hammer.

LEARNING CIRCLE ACTIVITY

1. Show a picture of Saturn.
2. Notice the rings of Saturn. What are the rings made of? After the children respond, explain that the rings are made of ice and rock.
3. Give each child a paper bag.
4. Go outside to collect rocks in different sizes. Explain that the Earth's rocks are similar to the rocks in Saturn's rings.
5. Have everyone bring their rocks to the Learning Circle.
6. Mix the crushed ice and rocks in a pan. Let each child feel the rings of Saturn!

PLUTO

MATERIALS

A pan of water.

PREPARATION

Freeze the pan of water.

LEARNING CIRCLE ACTIVITY

1. Explain that Pluto is the smallest planet. It is so small that some people are not sure that it is a planet! What else could Pluto be? Encourage a Brainstorm of ideas.
2. Show the pan of frozen water. Have everyone feel the ice. This is what Pluto feels like. It is so far from the Sun that it receives no heat. It is an icy ball!

THE PLANETS

MERCURY

MATERIALS

Playdough, small rocks.

PREPARATION

Gather the rocks.

LEARNING CIRCLE ACTIVITY

1. Give each child some playdough and a few rocks.
2. Have each child flatten their playdough. This is the surface of Mercury.
3. Each child pushes the rocks into their playdough.
4. Then they remove the rocks. Notice the holes that remain. The surface of Mercury is covered with holes called craters. Rocks from space have hit Mercury many times.

JUPITER

MATERIALS

A bowl of water, food dye.

PREPARATION

None

LEARNING CIRCLE ACTIVITY

1. Fill a large bowl with water. This is the surface of Jupiter.
2. Have everyone put their finger in the water. Explain that Jupiter is not solid like the Earth. You cannot step on it! It is a ball of gas.
3. Drop different colors of food dye into the water. Watch the colors swirl! This is the atmosphere of Jupiter. Explain that Jupiter is covered with multi colored clouds swirling storms above the surface of Jupiter.

MATERIALS FOR EXPANDING KNOWLEDGE

A picture of Jupiter.

EXPANDING KNOWLEDGE

Show a picture of Jupiter and its mysterious red spot. It moves around the planet. What do you think it could be? Some people think it could be a giant storm.

Jupiter has sixteen Moons! Have everyone count to sixteen. How many Moons does the Earth have?

MARS

MATERIALS

Butcher paper, paint, paintbrushes, tape.

PREPARATION

Secure a large sheet of butcher paper on a wall.

LEARNING CIRCLE ACTIVITY

1. Explain that on Mars the soil is red. Great dust storms cause the sky to look red.
2. Paint a Mars Mural! Have everyone paint grass, flowers, trees, animals, and houses on the butcher paper. Paint the sky red!
3. Do you think a red sky would look pretty? If you could change the color of the Earth's sky, what color would it be?

PREHISTORIC MURAL

MATERIALS

Butcher paper, tape, felt pens, crayons, a dinosaur coloring book, red crepe paper, scissors, fake fur, egg shells.

PREPARATION

Secure a large sheet of butcher paper on a wall. Draw a large volcano at one end of the butcher paper and a large prehistoric man at the other end. Tape a piece of fake fur across the prehistoric man's chest. Draw a lake on the Mural. Tape egg shells on the Mural!

LEARNING CIRCLE ACTIVITY

1. Give each child a selection of felt pens and have them draw tall grass, trees, and strange looking ferns on the Mural.

2. Have everyone color the Mural.
3. Tear out pages of a dinosaur coloring book and tape them on a wall.
4. Each child chooses a dinosaur picture to color and tape on the Mural.
5. Have everyone cut red crepe paper into streamers and tape them onto the volcano for lava.
6. Explain to the children that the dinosaurs came first and then the prehistoric people. Refer to the Mural many times while you are learning about prehistoric life.

DINOSAUR EGG GAME

MATERIALS

White posterboard, felt pens, a large bowl, sand, eggs, dinosaur stickers.

PREPARATION

Draw a large mother dinosaur on a posterboard. Place a bowl full of sand near the mother dinosaur. Boil eggs, one for each child, and place a dinosaur sticker on each one. Print a dinosaur Brainstorm question on the back of each egg. Dinosaur Brainstorm questions can include the following.

If dinosaurs were alive today, would that be good? Why?

What kind of dinosaur would you like to be?

If you had a dinosaur for a pet, where would it sleep?

If you were as big as a dinosaur, what would be hard to do?

What do you think a dinosaur did for fun?

What do you think a dinosaur would enjoy eating, if it lived today?

How was life different when dinosaurs lived on the Earth?

What do you think dinosaurs thought about?

What would be a good name for a dinosaur?

What color do you think dinosaurs were?

What kind of noise do you think a dinosaur made?

What would you miss the most, if you lived at the time of the dinosaurs?

LEARNING CIRCLE ACTIVITY

1. Place the eggs, question-side down, in the middle of the Learning Circle.
2. Explain that the mother dinosaur has lost her eggs!
3. Each child, in turn, chooses an egg, answers the Brainstorm question, and places it in the bowl of sand, sticker-side up, returning it to its mother.
4. At the end of the day, the children can take their egg home and share the Brainstorm question with their families.

A DINOSAUR STORY

MATERIALS

None

PREPARATION

None

LEARNING CIRCLE ACTIVITY

1. Read the Dinosaur Story to the children until they become familiar with the contents.
2. When the children know the story, leave out the underlined words.
3. See who can remember the omitted words.

The Dinosaur Story

We have learned many things about dinosaurs. Baby dinosaurs came from <u>eggs</u>.

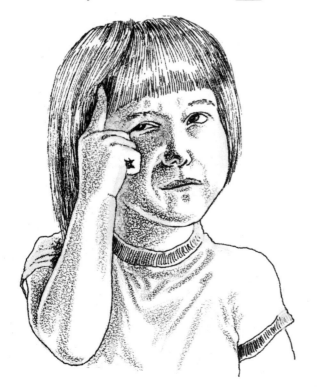

Some dinosaurs ate <u>plants</u>. Some dinosaurs ate <u>meat</u>. Some dinosaurs were <u>giant</u>! Others were as small as <u>chickens</u>. The word dinosaur means "<u>terrible lizard</u>."

The Brachiosaurus was the heaviest of all the dinosaurs. This dinosaur could move more easily in <u>water</u> and weighed as much as ten <u>elephants</u>. The Diplodocus was the longest dinosaur. It was as long as six <u>cars</u>. The king of the dinosaurs was the <u>Tyrannosaurus</u>. It was as tall as a <u>telephone pole</u> and ate <u>meat</u>! The other dinosaurs were afraid of the Tyrannosaurus because it could bite through <u>bone</u>. The Stegosaurus could fit inside a <u>house</u>. The back of the Stegosaurus was covered with many <u>plates</u>. The Brontosaurus was called the Thunder Lizard. When Brontosaurus walked, it sounded like <u>thunder</u>. The Trachodon was a plant eater with 2,000 <u>teeth</u>. Its bill looked like the bill of a <u>duck</u>. The Iguanodon had very sharp <u>claws</u>. To help keep its balance, it used its thick, heavy <u>tail</u>. The Pteranodon had very long wings. When it stretched them out, they were as long as <u>five</u> children, standing with their arms stretched out.

There are no more dinosaurs on the Earth. They are <u>extinct</u>, but it is fun to think about <u>dinosaurs</u>!

A PREHISTORIC PLAY

MATERIALS

None

PREPARATION

Learn the play.

LEARNING CIRCLE ACTIVITY

1. Have the entire class act out a day in the life of prehistoric people.
2. No props are necessary, only imaginations!
3. Perform the play indoors or outdoors. A suggested play.

   The day begins by gathering nuts, berries and eggs, then branches to build a cave. After everyone has finished building the cave they hunt for rocks and sticks. Then they sit in a circle and rub rocks against sticks, to make hunting tools.

(Choose some of the children to be Wooly Mammoths and have them wandering in a corner. The rest of the children are hunters.) The hunters rub two sticks together to make a fire and to light their torches to hunt with at dark. The hunters hold up their torches and herd the Mammoths into a muddy area. When the hunters throw their spears, the Mammoths fall to the floor. The hunters cut the skin off the Mammoths and hang the pieces on a tree branch to dry. They cut off chunks of meat and sling these over their shoulders to take back to their cave.

Back at the cave, the hunters cook the meat over the fire and eat with their fingers! Then they find a comfortable place to sleep.

WISH MACHINE

MATERIALS

Butcher paper, tape, felt pens, crayons, red felt material, a long paper tube from wax or Christmas wrapping paper, a small box, marbles, scissors, various classroom objects as suggested by the children.

PREPARATION

Secure a large sheet of butcher paper on a wall. Draw a large rectangle, three feet by six feet, on the paper using a black felt pen. Cut a heart shape and a circle from red felt material.

LEARNING CIRCLE ACTIVITY

1. Talk about the word invention. If you went home and made a pencil, would you have invented it? No! Somebody else has already invented it. If you made up a game, would you have invented it? Yes! You were the very first person to think of the game.
2. Explain that everyone is going to invent a Wish Machine.
3. Ask each child to name an object in the classroom that will help to create the Wish Machine.
4. Gather the objects.
5. Every child attaches their object on the Wish Machine Mural.
6. Everyone colors around the objects to add color to the Machine.
7. The teacher adds the final touches to make the Wish Machine work. Tape a red felt circle on the Machine and label it Start.
8. Tape a red felt heart on the Machine.
9. Tape a long paper tube on the Machine slanting downward with a small box taped at the bottom of it.
10. To start the Machine, have a child make a wish. The child then pushes the Start button, rubs the felt heart, and drops a marble down the tube. When the marble lands in the box, the wish is in the Machine.
11. Have everyone make a wish! Leave the Wish Machine on the wall for two weeks. Encourage the children to continue to make wishes. Encourage them to bring wishes from their families.

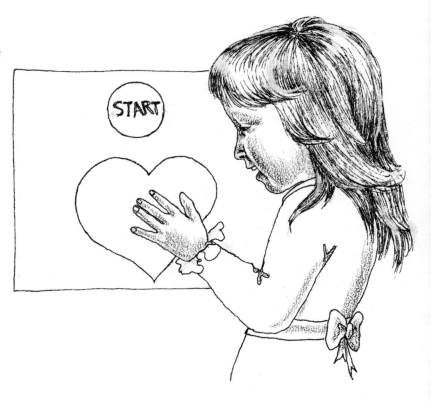

IMAGINATION INVENTIONS

MATERIALS

Various objects such as a sponge, a small ball, a spoon, a pillow, or a milk carton.

PREPARATION

Gather the objects.

LEARNING CIRCLE ACTIVITY

1. Place an object in the middle of the Learning Circle.

2. Can this object be made into something new and different? Encourage a Brainstorm of ideas. For example, a sponge could have wheels and be a sponge car for the bathtub. A marshmallow could be painted and hung as a Christmas decoration.
3. Try a different object each day!

FLOOR MACHINES

MATERIALS

Various objects such as straws, paper plates, crayons, strings of yarn, plastic forks, popsicle sticks, and pennies.

PREPARATION

Gather the objects.

LEARNING CIRCLE ACTIVITY

1. Place a selection of objects in front of every child.
2. Each child creates a design on the floor using the objects in front of them.
3. Everyone names their Machine and explains what it does!

MINIATURE WISH MACHINES

MATERIALS

Shoe boxes, small paper tubes, paint, paintbrushes, red felt material, sticky stars, glitter, scissors, marbles, glue.

PREPARATION

Cut hearts and circles from red felt material. Gather the objects.

LEARNING CIRCLE ACTIVITY

1. Give each child a shoe box or have them bring one from home.
2. The children paint their boxes and glue on a felt heart and circle.
3. Print the word Start above the circles.
4. Add sticky stars and glitter.
5. Cut two holes in the boxes on opposite sides, one hole slightly above the other.
6. Fit the paper tubes through the openings.
7. Give each Child a marble and have them make a wish.
8. The children catch the marble as it falls down the tube.
9. The children can take their Wish Machines home to share with their families.

THE CREATIVE COOK

MATERIALS

White posterboard, green posterboard, magazines, scissors, black felt pen, tape.

PREPARATION

Draw a large circle on a green posterboard. This is the salad bowl lined with lettuce. Draw horizontal lines across a white posterboard. This is a refrigerator with shelves.

LEARNING CIRCLE ACTIVITY

1. The children cut out food pictures from magazines. Cut out the usual salad ingredients and silly ingredients such as fish, peanut butter, honey, muffins, cookies, gum, pizza, and spaghetti!

2. Have the children tape their pictures on the refrigerator shelves.
3. At the Learning Circle have each child choose a food picture from the refrigerator and place it in the large green circle.
4. When everyone has had a turn, look at the salad! Think of a name for the original salad.
5. Create a different salad with a new name.

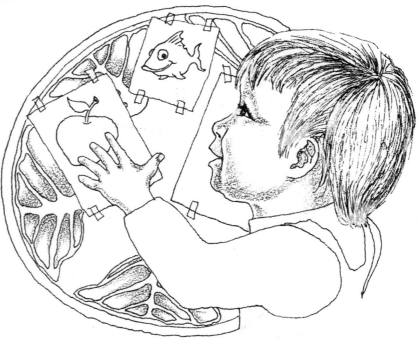

INDEX